PLANK-ON-FRAME-MODELS

Photo

THE BRIGANTINE "LEON".
(302 Tons)
Built at Laurvig, Norway, in 1880.
Port of Registry, Porsgrund.

[*Frontispiece*

PLANK-ON-FRAME MODELS

AND

Scale Masting and Rigging

BY

HAROLD A. UNDERHILL

A.M.I.E.S.

VOLUME I.

SCALE HULL CONSTRUCTION

With Plans and Sketches by the Author

GLASGOW

BROWN, SON & FERGUSON, LTD., Nautical Publishers

4-10 DARNLEY STREET

First Edition	–	1958
Reprinted	–	1962
Reprinted	–	1966
Reprinted	–	1968
Reprinted	–	1971
Reprinted	–	1974
Reprinted	–	1978
Reprinted	–	1981
Reprinted	–	1985
Reprinted	–	1991
Reprinted	–	1994
Reprinted	–	2001
Reprinted	–	2006

ISBN 0 85174 186 X / ISBN 978-0-85174-186-4

©2006—BROWN, SON & FERGUSON, LTD., GLASGOW, G41 2SD
Printed and Made in Great Britain

INTRODUCTION

AS originally planned this book was to have been published as a single volume, but the ever rising cost of production made it evident that to do so would result in it becoming too costly, and it was therefore decided to divide it into two.

The text has been written round the building of one of my own models, the brigantine Leon, following it through from the use of plans to the final mounting on the base ready for the glass case. This particular model has however not been slavishly followed, for where subsequent work or previous models have proved better technique, this has been quoted, in fact alternative methods of making the various components are included throughout.

This model belongs to what for the want of a better term I will call the "scale construction" class, in which the internal timbering follows in close detail that of the prototype vessel, but other and more simple methods have also been described, and although the example chosen represents a ship of the smaller type, the same construction will apply to vessels such as full-rigged ships and barques.

I have always held that to produce a first class model it is not sufficient merely to have good plans of the vessel being built, they must be backed up by a good understanding of the full-size prototype of the class, and I have therefore described full-size practice alongside details of the model, which broadens the scope for the modelmaker to apply his own methods to achieve the same results, should he wish to do so.

The obvious point at which to divide this book into two volumes is at the end of the last chapter dealing with scale hull construction, carrying over to Volume II the mast and spar making, mast "ironwork" and all rigging, and this has been done. The main difficulty has been to decide what to do with those sections dealing with special light weight construction for sailing models and power craft, and the chapter on clinker construction. Clearly the best place would have been in the first volume, but to have done so would have defeated the whole object of dividing the book, since it would have placed 75 per cent. of the subject matter under one cover. For that reason these two sections have been carried over to Volume II. This is not an entirely satisfactory arrangement, since some of the basic principles, such as the use of plans and the setting out and run of the planking, apply equally well to all methods of construction, from the glass case model with scale framing to the light weight sailer – and therefore Volume II will of necessity have to refer back to this for some items of detail.

The book has been written from the angle of the builder with limited tools and facilities, since my own model was built immediately after the war when I myself was in just that position, lacking both tools and workshop. However the construction used would have been just the same even though a fully equipped workshop had been available, but of course a good bench is always better than a poor table, and the wider the range of tools the greater the pleasure to be obtained from using them.

GLASGOW,   HAROLD A. UNDERHILL.
1958.

CONTENTS

ILLUSTRATIONS

List of Photograph

List of plates

CHAPTER I

PLANS AND PRELIMINARIES

I HAVE always been blessed, or cursed, with a "one-track mind", and my earliest recollections are of cardboard and knitting needle square-riggers battling with the heavy seas of an eiderdown quilt, but the first real impact with a serious model came to a small boy who, some 50 and years ago, discovered a beautiful little ship in the window of an antique dealer's shop, and thereafter made daily pilgrimages to gaze at it until at last it vanished to be seen no more, no doubt as the result of having been sold. I mourned its loss, but I now hope that it found a good and safe home, and is still in existence. That little ship belonged to the class I later learned to recognize as "Prisoner-of-war models", but the point which made the greatest impression on my young mind was the fact that it had "real planks" in the hull. I admired and coveted the model as a whole, but always came back to those "planks", and at home I spent many hours making sketches of their sweeps and curves. Today I cannot say whether she was a three-decker or frigate, but my admiration for her construction remains vividly in my mind. After each of those pilgrimages I came away vowing that one day I would myself own a model with "real planks" in the hull, and perhaps it was as well that I did not then know it would be about 80 years before that fond hope was satisfactorily realized.

After seeing that model in the shop window, none of the model ships which were a standing order for all Christmas and birthday presents, ever satisfied me. None of them had a "built" hull, and most of them I ultimately ruined in childish attempts to carve, scratch, paint or otherwise represent planking. However all this was not really a waste of time or models, for it taught me a lot about hull forms, and long before I was old enough to be articled to a drawing office I was quite at home on the board.

Even during the 1914-18 war, when serving abroad as a young sub-altern in a mounted regiment, I carried with me two books on my favourite subject, wood construction, one of which was discovered in my section limber by a senior officer during a snap roadside inspection, and ended its days in the Flanders mud at the bottom of a shell hole! The other, fortunately, I had always carried in my saddle bag where it escaped detection, to be read and re-read in muddy shelters, bivouacs and horse-lines. By

1

the end of the war the days of wooden shipbuilding were over, even small ships were being turned out in iron and steel, so it is not surprising that my spare time hobby should turn in the direction of modelling small wood-built craft.

For some reason or other the plank-built model has always been regarded with a certain amount of awe, even today when the standard of craftsmanship in sparetime model building is so much higher than it was some 40 years ago, there is still a tendency to regard such models as being beyond the ability of the ordinary man, while many of the older books on model building create the impression that only the master craftsman, with a skill amounting almost to genius, should give the matter second thoughts. Such books either elaborate on the supposed difficulties, or alternatively treat the subject so lightly as to be of no use to the beginner.

There was perhaps some excuse for this outlook half a century ago, for I have been looking over some of my old volumes of *The Model Engineer*, which go back to the year 1901, and I am rather amazed at some of the crude and out-of-scale models which are quite highly praised in its pages. At this period the *Model Engineer* was, I think, the only periodical devoted exclusively to model work. For some reason the railway models of the period are all far ahead of the marine models in the matter of scale and truth to prototype, while much the same may also be said about the workmanship. It is only in relatively recent years that the non-professional model builder has paid much attention to scale and detail in his model ships, or that the square-rigger has been used as the prototype.

I think the late Mr. Percival Marshall was perhaps the first to appreciate the interest there was in this type of ship if only the necessary information could be made available to the model maker, for it was in 1922, after a chat about some of my own early models, that he asked me to produce a set of scale drawings for a square-rigger. These were put on the market, the first time such drawings had been offered to the public, and immediately proved him to be right, there was an interest in such models. Those drawings were plans of a *model*, with all gear and detail simplified, and they fully met the demands of the time, but today, after over 1000 different model plans have come off my board, I no longer produce drawings of models, but plans of the original ships with as much detail as it is possible to obtain from the yard drawings or other sources. This I think clearly indicates the advance which has been made in the standard of craftsmanship of the non-professional model maker.

Of course the improvement in scale and detail has gone hand in hand with this improved standard of workmanship, particularly in the case of working models, not only in their external details, but also hull proportions. The deep out-of-scale hulls of the early part of the century were largely the result of the method of construction used. Most of these models were carved out of the solid block, frequently leaving several inches of solid timber at either end, and almost always with the bottom and sides 3/4 in. or 1 in. thick, so that they carried a lot of deadweight in the wrong places before their power plant, or ballast in the case of sailing models, was installed. It is not surprising that their hulls had to be enlarged much out of scale to carry it.

Both metal-plated and plank-on-frame hulls are so light and strong that there is no need to build them out of scale, even when intended for working models, since there is plenty of buoyancy to carry either power plant or ballast, while in the the case of a sailing ship the latter can be carried sufficiently low down in the hull to eliminate the need for unsightly deep fin keels. I have built and sailed plank-on-frame top's'l schooners without any form of fixed ballast whatever, but of that more later in Vol. II.

The idea that plank-on-frame construction is extremely difficult and therefore limited to a few super-men is one to which I do not subscribe, and I hope that by the end of this book the reader will be of the same opinion. I fail to see that the more simplified form as used for working models, either sail or power, offers any greater difficulty than say the laminated model, while there can be no doubt that it requires less hard work and provides more interest. The fully framed showcase model is more complicated than the working model, but in my opinion the only essential is that one should be out to enjoy *building* the model and not merely interested in seeing the finished product, in fact for me the real pleasure is in the work of building, rather than the model when complete. For this class of model one must be willing to scrap any component which, either through accident or lack of skill, is not quite right, and not try to "make it do". There I think is the only secret of the successful plank-built model, for there is no chance of rubbing down with sandpaper any bumps or irregularities which may have been left on frames or planking, but providing one is willing to take this little extra care, there is nothing in this type of model which is beyond the powers of the most ordinary model maker.

There are two great differences between the planked model and either the laminated or the solid model, and both are greatly to the advantage of the former. First I would place the actual work of construction. In either the laminated or solid block model many hours of hard work are required before one sees anything even remotely resembling a ship, whereas in the case of the fully framed model, built the right way up, one has a finished component, a part of a real ship, the right way up, one has a finished component, a part of a real ship, almost from the word "go". The keel is cut and can be laid on the building blocks or jig, just as it would be in a shipyard; it is the finished article, complete in itself. The stem and stern posts are made and fitted and one more stage is complete, so with each period you can see a real ship grow under your hands. No matter at what point you may stop work, you have a number of finished components either assembled or ready for assembly, just as you might have seen at the end of any working day in a shipyard of half a century ago, and so it continues until the last deck plank is laid and the last section of the rail fitted on top of the bulwark.

My second point would be that of building facilities. The solid and laminated models both require a substantial bench, or at least a good strong table to use as a bench, together with some means of holding the model during shaping, to say nothing of the quantity of shavings and chips produced from the operation. The "built" model on the other hand involves no heavy work whatever, requires only the lightest tools, and produces scarcely any mess. Owing to the post war conditions I had no workshop of any kind when building my fully-framed model of the brigantine *Leon*, which will be one of the models described in this book. She was built from keel to truck on a green-baize folding card table—and folding is the operative word, since it tried to perform that feat at most inconvenient times—in a room with a carpet extending right out to the walls, while my entire tool kit would pack into a pocket size box.

The heaviest material used was about 1/4 in. x 1/4 in. for square section stuff, and 3/8 in. x 1/8 in. for flats, for which a small jeweller's saw about 6 in. long was the largest needed. Of course the work would have been greatly simplified if carried out in a proper workshop, or even on a kitchen table, but my point is that this model did not suffer greatly as the result of the unconventional "workshop" used. This "workshop" was in fact a piece of laminated plywood about the size of the top of the table and fitted with a 2 in. "coaming" round three sides, rather like an old-fashioned pastry board, which kept the chips "on the island" instead of down on the carpet. This board, complete with tools and model on its building jig, was simply put away in a cupboard at the end of each evening's work. What laminated or solid model could have been built under such circumstances?

Perhaps I should mention the kind of tools used in building this particular model, although I would stress that had a workshop been available I would no doubt have made better use of others for some of the jobs, and in so doing improved the model slightly here and there, but the following will at least show that such a model can in fact be built with the minimum of equipment.

I obtained all my timber in either flats or squares of various sizes, some from hobby shops and others out of many years accumulation in my "junk box", so that I had no ripping-down to do, and therefore my largest cutting tool was the jeweller's saw already mentioned. Next came a small fretsaw using about a 4 in. blade, for which I have a strong frame which allowed it to be used like a hacksaw with the handle above instead of below the work. In use the items to be cut out were held on a thick block of wood, which allowed sufficient clearance above the table for a full stroke of the saw. I brought two chisels in from my tool box, one about 1/2 in. and the other 1/8 in. and although more were available where they came from I did not need to fetch them. I had a full range of warding files of all shapes and sections; twist drills ftom about 1/8 in. down to the smallest I could obtain, No. 80, and one or two small pin-chucks. I also have a small dentist's portable electric drill about the size of a pocket torch, which was very useful but in no way essential, in fact most of my drilling was done by means of the pin-chucks. A very small hand vice and a small iron plane, 3 in. long, completed the outflt used on the "workshop". I also have two draw-plates for making dowels, which for the sake of convenience I used in a vice clamped to the office table, but which could just as well have been used by hand on my folding table. I think it will be agreed that no other form of timber-built model of this size could have been made with such tools or under such circumstances.

The point on which I most disagree with such books as I have read on the subject of plank-built-models, is that one is usually told to make the various components of say a frame, and then join them together, but my own experience of this method has been that the finished frame is usually a fraction wide or narrow at the top, due to some slight inaccuracy in the angle of one of the joints. This no doubt is an admission of lack of skill on my part, but it requires the angle of a joint to be only the smallest fraction out of truth to throw a frame out of line. I always reverse this procedure by making all the joints in a frame, or other component, before cutting to shape, so that any little inaccuracy in jointing in no way effects the finished product, in fact the angle of the joint is to a large extent unimportant. I think many would-be plank-built model makers have been discouraged before starting work by thoughts of having to work to such fine limits in making joints, or disheartened at a later stage by finding frames running out of true.

Before going on with the actual construction of the first model, it may be as well to look at the different methods of building available. For this purpose models can be divided into three main categories. First there is the showcase model with some or all of the planking omitted below the waterline to show the timbering. Next the showcase model which is fully planked from keel to rail, with all the internal work hidden, and lastly the sailing model in which plank-on-frame construction is used solely for its extreme lightness and better sailing qualities, or in the case of power craft, carrying capacity.

Under the first heading the only possible answer in the case of merchant ships is to reproduce the framing as in the full size vessel, although for warship models one has the alternative of the conventional framing as used in the old Navy Board models, However as this book is limited to merchant craft, the latter will not be described.

The second class of model offers a wide range of styles, it can either be fully framed and planked over; the frames cut out in one piece with the beams, the frames may be left solid like bulkheads, or one may even plank on top of a solid hull. In warship models where one can see into the upper decks through the gun-ports, one can make the hull solid below the level of the lower deck, with frames let into this and carried up to the rail. Personally I have never favoured this type of construction, which to me seems to have most of the disadvantages of the solid block model, with the additional disadvantage of having to blend the frames of the topsides into it. Both this type and the entirely solid hull planked over involve all the hard work of the solid hull, which is a thing I like to avoid, and at the same time lack all the pleasure of seeing the ship grow on the stocks, which to me is one of the great joys of the model wooden ship. This latter may also be said to apply to all the "short-cut" styles of building planked models, such as the solid bulkhead or the frames sawn out from a single piece of wood, usually plywood. I had one model, to which I will refer later, built on plywood frames, and I will never again use this method, for having occasion many years later to remove some "spongy" strakes, I found that the frames had opened up all along the junction between two of the plys, where the plank fixings had acted as wedges and forced them apart.

One thing which must be remembered if using any of these "simplified framing" techniques, is that even though the framing may not be visible in the finished job, the plank fixings will, and therefore the full number of cut-out frames or solid bulkheads should be fitted, otherwise the plank fixings will be too far apart for scale proportions. It is not much use making a perfect scale model in all external details if one can see at a glance that the internal framing is at 10 ft. instead of 2 ft. centres. This of course will not show if the hull is thickly coated with paint, but there seems little purpose in planking the hull of a showcase model if the work is to be hidden under a coat of paint, and one thing is certain, if the plank seams show, so will the fixings.

In my own model of *Leon* I struck the half-way mark between the fully planked and the half planked model. I placed the ship on blocks as she might be if hauled out for repairs, and left off enough planking from one side to show the internal framing, leaving a few of the "old" planks as well as "new material" alongside the slip, which together with the builders' staging and shipyard workers offers sufficient excuse for the missing planks. She is in fact having some doubtful strakes removed and replaced, a perfectly normal procedure with wooden ships.

Finally we have the sailing model: in this the frames should be as light and simple as possible, spaced as far apart as the thickness of the planking will allow, and for this I think the bent frame is the best, following a similar construction to that used in first-class model racing yachts, although modified to suit the different hull form of the merchant sailing ship or power hull, as will be described in Vol. II.

I suppose the greatest difficulty likely to be experienced by the average model builder on his first attempt at a plank-on-frame job, will be the fact that the Lines Drawing will have to be adapted to suit this type of construction, since he will have to make his own templates for the frames, but this is not the formidable task it may at first appear, in fact it is really quite simple. The most common frame spacing for a model of a merchant ship will be what is termed "room and space", which means that the space between any two frames is equal to the thickness of the frame, this applies whether the frames are single or double *Sketch No.* 1. The two dimensions of the material forming a frame are known as the "moulded" and "sided" sizes *Sketch No.* 2.

It will be obvious that with frames so closely spaced it would be impossible for any Lines Drawing to show the shape of them all, since the variation between one frame and the next, particularly in the centre of the ship, would be so slight that all the lines in the Body Plan would just run together and become a solid mass. For this reason the cross-stations on a Lines Drawing are usually placed at intervals convenient for the displacement calculations and may have no relation to the position of the frames, and even if they do fall on any of the frame stations, there will still be quite a number of frames to be filled in between them. All the same, whether they fall on any of the frame stations or not, all the information necessary for finding the shape of every frame in the ship is already in the Lines Drawing and can be found by a little of the most elementary draughtsmanship, and with no other instruments than a pair of compasses and a straightedge.

At this stage we will forget the thickness of the frames and the method of deciding the frame spacing, and confine our efforts to "lifting" the frame shapes from an ordinary Lines Drawing in which the frames do not correspond with the station lines. On your Lines Drawing, the Sheer Plan (showing the side view of the ship) and Half-breadth Plan (showing the shapes of the various waterlines) will be placed one above the other, with the station lines "fairing" through. We will assume that your frames are to be at 1/2 in. centres, so along the uppermost waterline in the Sheer Plan mark off 1/2 in. intervals on either side of the midship station, do the same along the centreline of the Half-breadth Plan, and then rule lines through these dots right across both Sheer Plan and Half-breadth Plan, just as the station lines of the original Lines Drawing do. These lines you have just drawn represent one face of each of your frames. At the extreme end of

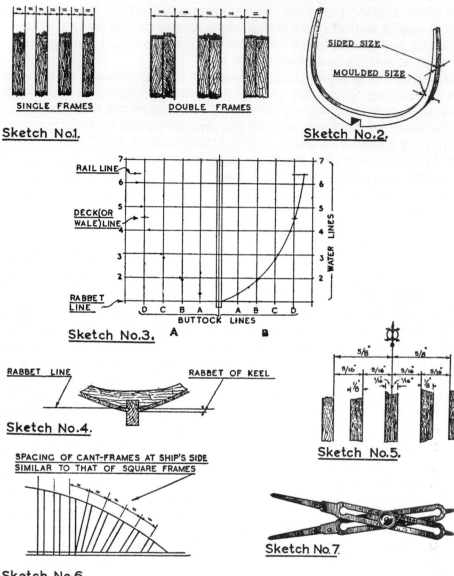

SINGLE FRAMES

DOUBLE FRAMES

Sketch No.1.

SIDED SIZE

MOULDED SIZE

Sketch No.2.

RAIL LINE

DECK (OR WALE) LINE

RABBET LINE

BUTTOCK LINES

WATER LINES

Sketch No.3.

A   B

RABBET LINE   RABBET OF KEEL

Sketch No.4.

5/8"   5/8"

5/16" 5/16" 5/16" 5/16"

1/8"   1/16" 1/16" 1/8"

Sketch No.5.

SPACING OF CANT-FRAMES AT SHIP'S SIDE
SIMILAR TO THAT OF SQUARE FRAMES

Sketch No.6.

Sketch No.7.

Sketch No.8.

the ship where the waterlines taper into the stem, frames fitted at right angles to the centreline, like those just drawn, would have too much bevel on their outer surfaces to be of much use, so at this point the frames will be arranged at varying angles to the centreline and are known as cant-frames, but these can be ignored for our present purpose which is merely to show how the shape of a frame, either cant or square, can be lifted off the Lines Drawing.

The next step is to make a tracing of the "grid" of the Body Plan, that is to say, the vertical centreline, the vertical buttock lines (A.B.C.D. in *Sketch No.* 3 and the horizontal waterlines, drawn full width of the Body Plan. Place the needle of your compasses at the intersection of the centreline and the frame you wish to "lift", on the Half-breadth Plan, and measure to where this frame crosses the uppermost waterline. Place the needle of your compasses at the intersection of this waterline and the centreline on your tracing of the grid, and mark the distance on either side. Do this for each waterline in turn. Now move to the Sheer Plan, and from the base line, which will usually be the rabbet of the keel, or rabbet-line *Sketch No.* 4, measure up to where your frame crosses the first buttock line "A", *Sketch No.* 3 and transfer this to your tracing on both sides of the centreline. Do the same for the remaining buttock lines. Next measure from the rabbet line up to the rail and mark this on either side of your tracing, also from the rabbet line up to the deck line or the level of the wale according to the type of ship to be built, and transfer this to your tracing in the same way and rule lines right across. On these respective rail and deck lines mark off the width of the vessel at these levels as shown on the Half-breadth Plan, and your tracing will have a series of dots as shown in "A" *Sketch No.* 3. Join up the dots, as "B", and when this has been done on both sides, you have the proper outline of the frame you have selected. On this tracing you will now add the internal shape of the frame and also the bevel, but these points I will cover later, in the meantime I only wish to show how the various shapes are transferred from the Lines Drawing, on which they do not originally appear. Marking off the rail and deck or wale lines from the Sheer Plan is very important, for on the accuracy of these levels will depend the sweet run of the sheer of the ship.

Having outlined the general principle of lifting off the frame outline, we will now take this a stage further and show how the complete frame, including bevels, can be taken off, and for this purpose we will assume that we are building a model of the brigantine *Leon*, plans of which are published here. As a matter of fact in producing the Lines Drawing for this vessel I worked in the station lines so that they would fall on alternate frame stations, leaving only intermediate frames to be filled in. I also included full size drawings of each of the cant-frames, including bevels, but for the purpose of this book I propose to assume that such details are not available, and that we have to work them out as we go along, as would probably be the case for any other model.

We will assume that the Lines Drawing in possession of the model builder is drawn to the inside of the planking—in many cases it will not, but I deal with that later—in which case the rabbet line of the keel *Sketches No. 3 and* 4 will form the base line as already described. In *Leon*, a small merchant ship, the timbering is not quite "room and space", and on the size of model shown in the plans the sided size of the frames is 1/8 in. while the space between them is 3/16 in., making a total of 5/16 in., for a frame and the space to the next one, so the first task will be to rule lines across both Sheer Plan and Half-breadth Plan, 1/16 in. on either side of the midship station *Sketch No.* 5, which will represent the thickness, or sided size of the midship frame. Now on either side of the midship station on both Sheer Plan and Half-breadth Plan, set off points 5/16 in. apart, going right aft to the stern, but forward only to where the bow starts to taper in sharply, beyond which cant-frames will be required. In *Leon* this is station No. 3, as shown on the Lines Drawing *Plate No.* 1. One word of warning here, although it will not be needed by anyone used to setting out equal spaces such as this. When marking out these 5/16 in. spaces, do not measure the first 5/16 in., then move the rule along and measure the next, in this way you are almost certain to develop a slight "creep" in your measurements. Hold the end of your rule on the midship line and then mark off 5/16 in.; 5/8 in.; 15/16 in; $1\frac{1}{4}$ in.; $1\frac{9}{16}$ in.; and so on, keeping the end of the rule fixed on the starting point all the time, in this way, should you make a fractional error on any of the measurements, it will be corrected by the next, and not carried forward as would be the case if the rule were moved along from point to point. In the same way, do not use a pair of dividers or compasses to "step" off the distances, for it is surprising how one can get out of truth by such a method. It only needs the point of the needle to find a pin hole in the drawing board, or grain in the bench, to throw the spacing out, and this error will be carried forward.

Having ruled the lines representing the faces of the frames across both Sheer Plan and Half-breadth Plan, measure *forward* 1/8 in. of all lines in the fore part of the ship, and *aft* of all lines aft of the midship section, and rule these lines right across both plans. You now have the sided size of all frames, except the cants, drawn in on your plan, and it will be seen that all your frames in the forward part of the hull are forward of the station lines, and all those in the after body of the ship, aft of the station lines, the reason being that the ship tapers toward the ends, and you want to be able to trim the taper or bevel *off* the edges of your frames, not add it on.

Now that all the thwart-ship frames are drawn in, the cant-frames can be added. Your Lines Plan will show the thickness of the keel, but if this does not run back from the stem, then extend it as far as your last square frame. Now from the outer end of your last square frame as shown on the Half-breadth Plan, divide the outer line of the deck into spaces approximately equal to the spacing of the frames in the rest of the hull, i.e. 5/16 in. in the case of the 1/8 in. scale model of *Leon*. *Sketch No.* 6 and from these points draw in the cant frames so that their outer faces are about true to the run of the planking. The sketch referred to and *Plates No.* 1 *and* 2 will make this clear. These frames will of course not run right across the ship, but be fixed to the dead-wood—the solid timber joining the stem to the keel.

All the frames are now lined off on the plans, and the "drawing office" work is complete, so we are now ready to start on the actual construction of the model. Seen in print this "drawing office" stage may appear rather complicated, but, as the reader will find when he comes to put it into practice, it really is extremely simple, and when once the basic principle is understood it will not offer any difficulty.

However, before going on to the practical work, it may be as well to add a few words on the subject of building a model for which plans of the right scale are not available, and which have to be either enlarged or reduced. This, since the frames have to be lifted off the Lines Drawing in any case, offers no additional work, and it is as easy to enlarge or reduce the size during the construction of the model as to build to the same size as the drawings, for unlike the laminated or solid block model, it is extremely unlikely that there will be any moulds or templates which can be traced direct from the plans, except perhaps the curve of the stem.

If you do intend to work to a different scale to that of the plans, then it is well worth investing in a pair of draughtsman's proportional dividers, such as can be obtained from any shop dealing in drawing instruments. These dividers, *Sketch No.* 7, are double-ended and pivot on a central screw which slides along a graduated scale on the body of the instrument. Moving this screw up or down the scale varies the relative opening of the points at opposite ends. Different graduations are available, but the most common is that which indicates the number of times the wider end is greater than the smaller. Thus if the screw is set to "3" on the scale the ratio between the two ends will be 3 to 1, so that if the small end is opened to 1 in., the points of the other end will be 3 in. apart. The marking of the scale is however not really important, for any ratio, no matter how unusual, can always be obtained by trial and error. For example, if you should want a ratio of say $1^5/_8$ in. to 1 in., which is extremely unlikely, it is only a matter of setting the points of the small end to 1 in., and moving the screw along until those at the other end are at $1^5/_8$ in., and clamping it at that, after which any measurement taken by the small end will be reproduced $1^5/_8$ times larger at the other.

The use of this instrument in say enlarging your model is obvious, simply set the serew at the enlargement you require, measure from your plan with the small end, and set out the work with the other. If you are reducing the scale, then the dividers are used the other way round, measuring with the large end and setting off the work with the small. These dividers can also be of the greatest assistance in setting out the run of the planking, but of that more later.

I mentioned the stem as being something for which you would not have a full size template in the case of a model to a different scale to the plans, but if you can enlarge the frames, you can, obviously, enlarge the stem in the same way, the only difference being that it is not covered by a grid as in the case of the frames. However all you have to do is to rule a grid over the stem on the Sheer Plan, any kind of grid will do, you need not even measure it, for you will enlarge it by means of the proportional dividers, then take off all the vertical dimensions where the curve of the stem crosses the vertical lines and transfer them to the enlarged size on your new grid. Do the same with the horizontals, join up the dots and you have the enlarged outline of the stem. This same principle can of course be used for enlarging any curved surface throughout the whole plan, also in making deck fittings, etc., it is only a case of measuring them on the drawing with one end of the instrument, and setting them out directly on the material to be used with the other.

In the following chapters I will be describing several different methods of construction, such as single and double "built" frames, with either simple scarfed joints or full butt-chock connections, as well as the non-scale methods including laminated and bent frames in Vol. II. For my model of *Leon* I used single frames, in the ring-net boat shown in some photographs double frames, but the reader will of course understand that all these methods are within certain limits according to prototype, interchangeable. There is no reason why the reader should not build a model brigantine or schooner with double frames and a ship or barque with single, or vice versa, providing that she is to be planked over. If on the other hand he is leaving the timbering exposed then he will have to follow the construction used in the original if it is known. In the main however it will be open to him to use whichever type is most suitable to the materials available and the facilities he has for working.

It is of course also possible to combine some of these various methods in one hull, as for example that shown in *Fig.* 4. This model was to have been fully planked and decked, so that none of the internal work would have been visible in the finished job, and I did not attempt to reproduce scale framing. I used double frames just close enough to support the planking, but as this would have made the plank fixings much out of scale distance when seen from the outside, I ran light bent frames between them just to correct this. Unfortunately this hull was on the stocks at the outbreak of war and did not survive to be completed. Incidentally the deck beams were merely placed in position for the purpose of taking the picture, for as will be seen the deck-shelf had not at that time been fitted. I have already explained that for me the pleasure of model building is to see it grow as would a fullsize vessel, which explains the type of rough stocks being used for this model during the final stages.

I wish to acknowledge those photographs which have been lent for the purpose of illustrating models under construction, or complete. At the time I built my own models I had no thought of a book such as this, and not being in any way interested in photography, it did not even occur to me to keep a pictorial record of progress for any of them, therefore when I came to need such views all I could find was the picture recently referred to and the almost completed hull of *Leon* which forms the subject of *Fig. 17*. However for the brigantine, Professor H. Favez of Renens in Switzerland came to my rescue. I have known Professor Favez's really first class model work for many years, and when I explained my difficulty he at once offered me pictures of his own model of *Leon* under construction, for which I am very grateful.

These pictures are of particular interest, for not only do they show the model both in frame and complete, but they also illustrate how it is possible for two builders to approach the same job, and achieve the same results, by different methods. The following chapters will describe the building of my own model of this ship, and in some ways they will not agree with the pictures, yet as I have already said, the results will be the same, we both have a 1/8 in. scale model of *Leon* to show for our efforts. As an example of some of the differences, it will be seen that when planking the model, Professor Favez inverted it on a special jig and held the planks by means of large spring clamps, *Fig. 14*, whereas I left the model on the original building base the whole time, simply lifting it out of the jig and laying it on the table while actually fitting the planks, returning it to the jig after each period of work. To hold the planks during fitting I used a few simple home-made clamps when necessary, but in the main used the fingers of one hand to keep the planks in place while drilling the holes with the other. I like to have the model entirely free during planking, so that I can turn it this way and that, just as required to give the best approach to the particular job in hand, and also to be able to examine the model from all angles.

On the other hand it will be noticed that Professor Favez used the alternative built-up stern frame as used in my own model, and not the fashion-piece shown on the working drawings, but I was in constant touch with him during the building of his *Leon*, and passed on the amendments I had made in mine, these he followed. His method of finding the run of the planks was derived from some of the sketches now used in this book, but whereas I pinned the battens in position and only removed them as each was reached by the planking, he wired them on, and after marking out the run of the planks, removed several battens ahead of the planks as will be seen from the illustrations.

Mr. George MacLeod of Stornoway is an old friend and collaborator of mine, and a real artist in the building of perfect scale models, so I naturally turned to him for pictures of his *Zulu*, which I felt must be included in any book on plank-built models, even though its real aim was the larger merchant ship types. This model is now in The National Maritime Museum, Greenwich.

Mr. Jesus Bracamontes of Coyoacan, Mexico, is another model maker whose work I have admired, and the photographs of his model built from the *Leon* plans appeal to me on account of their general "Atmosphere". In many external details Mr. Bracamontes had departed from the true *Leon*: the boats in davits on either quarter, the brailed spanker, and the anchor in the fore shrouds are all foreign to the trading brigantine of this class, but the general appearance of the decks are just what they should be in such a vessel. These little brigantines were not training ships or men-of-war, with everything spick-and-span and all gear coiled to perfection, they were small merchant ships with very small crews, and so those odd coils of rope and other gear about the decks look just right. The gear is not coiled with mathematical precision, the coils look natural.

CHAPTER II

BUILDING THE FRAME

FOR this first model I propose to take my own model of the brigantine *Leon*, but before going into details I should perhaps say something about materials. Had this book been written before the 1939-45 war I would have specified the type of timber to be used for each job, but to do so now would be a waste of time, and perhaps dishearten the prospective builder if he thought he had to get this or that wood to make a proper job of any part of the model. Prior to the war one could walk into almost any good hobby shop and purchase first-class timber, usually available in cut sizes which were of the greatest assistance to the model shipbuilder. Flats ranged from about 1/8 in. x 1/16 in. up to say $2^{1}/_{2}$ in. x 1/4 in., squares from 1/16 in. x 1/16 in. to 1 in. x 1 in., and even if the exact size was not available, most places would rip it down for you. Timber sheets started at 1/32 in. thick and could be obtained in most of the better hardwoods.

Unfortunately those days are gone, at least for the present, and whereas it used to be possible to build a model to a specification, today one has to accept the best one can get and make it do. Under these circumstances I feel that it will be sufficient to say that the main thing in selecting timber for plank built models is to get something reasonably hard and very close in the grain. Timber which is either short or wavy in the grain, or open and coarse in texture is of no use for this class of work, short grained wood will not stand the bending and twisting which is necessary in planking, while a wavy grain will probably result in twisting in members which should remain dead straight.

If I had a free choice of material for this class of model I would place boxwood at the top of the list, it is beautiful timber to work and almost entirely free from grain, in fact it is often quite difficult to decide which way the grain is running. Like everything else, boxwood can vary in quality, although I do not think I have ever had a really bad piece. However from my rather limited experience of it, I think that the darker "golden" coloured wood works better than the paler stuff.

Next to boxwood I would place sycamore, and this is a material of which I have wider experience, having built quite a number of models using it throughout. This wood is, of course, almost pure white in colour, with rather more grain than boxwood, but often beautifully marked, which can be most effective when polished. Sycamore requires a little more care in selection than box, for it is possible to find pieces with a shaky grain, but in general the grain is sufficiently close to be worked in any direction. It is quite hard, yet the smaller sections bend well, and once bent will retain the set, a good feature for this class of model. I have used sycamore for planking and always have been very pleased with the result.

Pear is another wood which I believe gives good results, although I have no experience of it other than using a few small pieces for fittings. Many years ago I acquired two or three logs of well seasoned holly, which I had ripped down by a sawmill, and I found this very good material for carving, but the stuff I have is too wavy in grain to be much use for main construction work. Whether this is characteristic of the wood I do not know, for I have always tried to concentrate on sycamore or boxwood, and until 1939 always used one or the other.

When in 1946 I decided to build the model of *Leon* I went to the people who had always supplied me in the past, intending to get either box or sycamore, only to learn that they were unable to supply either. I returned home and examined my collection of "scrap" (although I would take a poor view of anyone else calling it that!). Fortunately I have always been something of a magpie where either bits of good timber or non-ferrous metal are concerned, for I am one of those people who refuse to have any ready made fittings on any of my models, and so small bits of material are always in demand. For this purpose I keep some old "tin trunks" into which every scrap of wood, brass or copper has been thrown, until over the years they have become full, and my timber collection ranges from bits about the size of a small nut, up to quite useful cuttings. Out of this collection I was able to raise sufficient sycamore to make most of the small components which go to building a model of this kind, which after all is another advantage of the "built" hull.

One thing I could not find in the scrap box was sufficient material for the planking, and after another search of the dealers, I had to accept some strips of 1/16 in. birch, which I found worked quite well although it lacks the finish obtainable on sycamore. The deck fittings, houses, etc., offered no difficulty, they all came out of bits from the scrap box. Incidentally I also did a bit of "trade" in boxwood folding rules, by offering anyone a new 3 ft. boxwood rule for an old one. The old pre-war rules were usually made of really first-class boxwood, whereas those turned out immediately after the war did not seem of the same quality. I got several old rules in this way, which were used for making blocks, etc.

For the masts and spars I was very fortunate in having some fine old straight grained yellow pine which came out of some old drawers picked up in a junk shop years ago. This incidentally is another good source of first-rate material, really old furniture, although not necessarily valuable, usually had the backs and bottoms of drawers made of yellow pine, a timber now rather difficult to get, and by the time such furniture has reached the "junk" stage, one can be certain that it is well seasoned. The stuff I had did not need ripping down, I simply split it and it was all ready for shaping up into the spar, so there is little risk that these spars will ever show any signs of twist.

The first stage of construction of the model will be to provide a good strong baseboard for which you will require a stout plank about four inches wider than the beam of the model, and about a foot longer. I found a piece of 3/4 in. laminated plywood ideal for this. This type of plywood, by the way, has three layers, the outer ones being thin flat sheets as in ordinary plywood, while the inner ply is made up of strips on edge *Sketch No. 8.* It is very strong and free from twist. If a good stiff board is not available, then get the best you can and strengthen it by means of 3/4 in. or 1 in. square rails on the under side. It is most important that this board shall not twist, for on it will depend the whole truth of the finished model. If the board twists, then the stem and stern posts of the model will not be in line.

Clean up the surface of the board, and strike a pencil line down the centre, taking care that it is dead straight. Now in the centre of the length of the board strike a line across it at right angles to the main centreline, and this will represent the centre of your midship frame. Care must be taken that this line is truly at right angles to the C/L, and personally I always set out these cross lines by means of compasses rather than trusting to a joiner's square running along the edge of the board, which might be slightly out. Now strike in the remaining cross lines on either side of this, representing the faces of the frames which you have drawn on your Lines Drawing. When all these are in, it is a good idea to go over them lightly with the point of a sharp tool run along the edge of a steel rule, and so scribe them into the wood, since in course of time the pencil lines will certainly be rubbed off. I also run in the outline of the boat, set off from the Half-breadth Plan, although this is not really necessary, but it is sometimes useful to be able to see at a glance just how much of the baseboard will be outside the width of the model at any one point.

This is not a book on full-size construction, but I think it is always an advantage to understand the basic principles of any prototype you may be building, after which you can either amplify or modify the detail reproduced in your model, according to its scale or purpose, so I will illustrate the various full-size components as I go along, followed by the description of my own model of *Leon.* This brigantine was of course a relatively small vessel, 302 tons gross, built in 1880 at Larvik, the name of her builder being unknown. Her dimensions were 110·7 ft. x 28·0 ft. x 13·2 ft. and her home port Porsgrund, while her history and fate I have described in *Deep-*

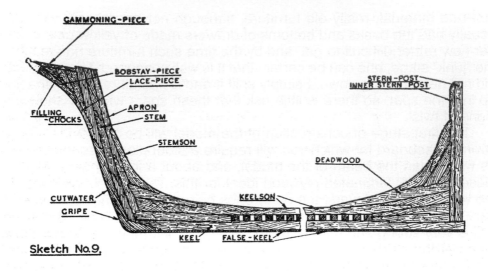

Sketch No.9.

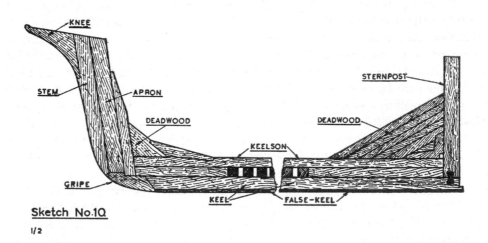

Sketch No.10

1/2

water Sail. My own model is to 1/8 in; scale. and as it was to be more or less fully planked, I very slightly modified the internal construction to the extent of making the stem and apron in one piece. Why I did this I really do not know, for I think making the apron separately would if anything have simplified the work. In most other models I have made these two components separately, and this may have been the explanation, I like to try everything once! The rest of the construction followed normal practice.

The construction of what might be described as the "backbone" of a wooden ship, i.e. Keel, Stem and Stern-post, followed the same broad principles in all vessels, but varied in matters of detail according to their size, country of origin, and builder. In this country the timber actually available in the yard at the time also played a part in deciding the size, and to some extent the shape, of the various components forming the whole. *Sketch No.* 9 has been taken from an old rough sketch, probably made out in the yard when looking over the timber, and seems to indicate a vessel of some 900 tons. Unfortunately there is nothing to identify either the vessel or builder. *Sketch No.* 10 is from the original builders' constructional plan of the American barquentine *Newsboy*, a vessel of 589 tons, built by Dickey Brothers of San Francisco in 1882. She was 168·0 ft. long x 38·0 ft. beam, with a depth of 13·9 ft. The difference between these is very striking and clearly indicates their respective countries of origin, although of course the matter of size also plays a part. American construction at this period always ran on more simple lines, both internally and externally, as can be seen by comparing the deck structures of the two countries. Ships built in the States were largely content with a match-board finish for their deckhouses, etc., while we continued to panel ours as long as timber was used in ship construction. As to the internal construction work, the answer probably lay in the fact that America had unlimited supplies of timber on the doorstep, while we had to import most of ours and make the best possible use of all we had, so shorter lengths were worked in wherever possible.

Now to the model. The first item to be taken in hand will be the keel, which on 1/8 in. scale is 1/4 in. deep x 5/32 in. moulded. Take a strip of hardwood, long enough to extend an inch or more beyond the overhang of the counter aft, and also out past the stemhead forward, and after making certain that it is dead-straight and free from twist, plane it down to the exact scantlings required and lay aside while the stem and stern-posts are taken in hand.

Leon has a form of "fiddle-head" bow, and for this a stem built in two pieces as shown on the plans is sufficient to take the grain in the right direction. For a bow having greater sweep, three pieces as shown in *Sketch No.* 11 would be preferable, but the exact arrangement will depend upon the curvature of the stem in the particular model being built, and is

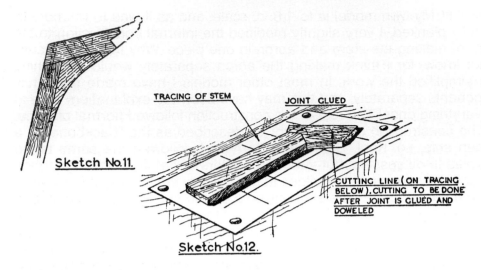

TRACING OF STEM

JOINT GLUED

Sketch No. 11.

CUTTING LINE (ON TRACING, BELOW). CUTTING TO BE DONE AFTER JOINT IS GLUED AND DOWELED

Sketch No. 12.

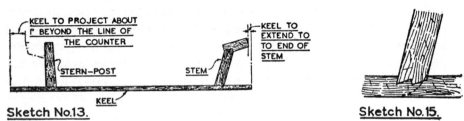

KEEL TO PROJECT ABOUT 1" BEYOND THE LINE OF THE COUNTER

KEEL TO EXTEND TO TO END OF STEM

STERN-POST

STEM

KEEL

Sketch No. 13.

Sketch No. 15.

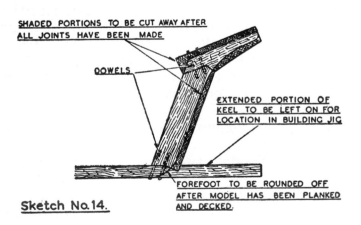

SHADED PORTIONS TO BE CUT AWAY AFTER ALL JOINTS HAVE BEEN MADE

DOWELS

EXTENDED PORTION OF KEEL TO BE LEFT ON FOR LOCATION IN BUILDING JIG

FOREFOOT TO BE ROUNDED OFF AFTER MODEL HAS BEEN PLANKED AND DECKED.

Sketch No. 14.

1/3

a matter for the discretion of the builder, the main point being to carry the grain round the stem as much as possible. This may not seem very important in a small scale model, but if it is to be either polished or clear varnished, then the run of the grain will be seen, and it is just one of those small points which are either right or wrong, so one may just as well have it right, even at the expense of a little extra trouble, although personally I do not regard such construction as extra *trouble*, rather as extra pleasure, for the joy of such a model is in the making.

Make a rough tracing of the complete stem and pin it down on a flat board, and on this lay two pieces of wood of suitable thickness and sufficient width to cover the drawing, and while in this state make the joint between the stem and the stemhead. This joint should then be glued, and the job left under a heavy weight until dry, *Sketch No*. 12, after which it can be dowelled, taking care that the dowels pass through the joint at points inside the finished stem and not in the portion to be cut away when it is finally shaped. I believe in making all such joints with the components lying flat on a level surface, and by putting a weight, such as an old flat-iron, on top, one is certain that everything will be square and true when lifted. The components will stick to the tracing, or any sheet of paper which is below them but this is all to the good, in fact as will be seen later in the book, I make a practice of glueing all such components to paper, and leaving the paper in position throughout the work on the assembly to strengthen it. The stern-post should be traced and cut out in the same way.

When the "roughs" of both stem and stern-post are ready, lay them, together with the keel, on the arrangement drawing, or constructional plan if one is available, and mark out the joints between these three components, taking care that the keel projects at either end as already mentioned. These joints can now be glued and the whole assembly left under a heavy weight until dry, after which the joints with the keel should be dowelled. This unit will now appear as *Sketch No*. 13. In *Leon* I made the simple joint between the stem and keel as shown in the plans and *Sketch No*. 14, but in a larger model a fully scarfed joint as *Sketch No*. 15 would be used.

This arrangement of scarfing the stem directly into the keel was common practice in smaller vessels, although in larger ships a separate gripe-piece was usually fitted, and in any vessel with a well rounded forefoot, absolutely necessary. *Leon's* forefoot is sharp and the direct scarf in order, while it has the added advantage of allowing the extension being left on the keel during construction, the object of which will be clear later.

While the joints in the keel, stem and stern-post assembly are drying, the "stocks" on which the model is to be built can be taken in hand. On either side of the centreline on the baseboard run another pencil line half the thickness of the keel away, representing the outer faces of the keel,

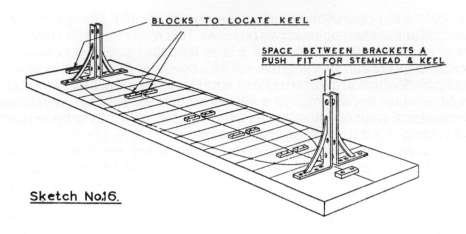

BLOCKS TO LOCATE KEEL

SPACE BETWEEN BRACKETS A
PUSH FIT FOR STEMHEAD & KEEL

Sketch No. 16.

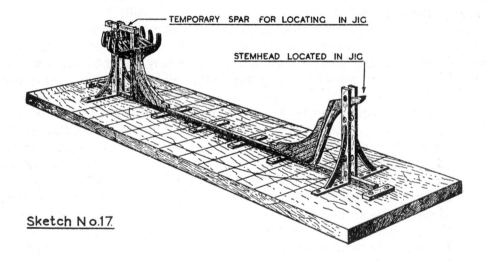

TEMPORARY SPAR FOR LOCATING IN JIG

STEMHEAD LOCATED IN JIG

Sketch No. 17.

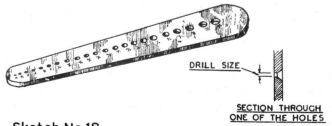

DRILL SIZE

SECTION THROUGH
ONE OF THE HOLES

1/4 Sketch No. 18.

then from a strip of 1/4" x 1/8" wood cut a number of lengths, each about 1" long. Glue or pin these to the board in pairs, one on either side of the keel lines, with their inboard ends just on the line, so that the keel will be a push-fit between them, and placed between the frame positions, as shown in *Sketch No.* 16. At either end of the baseboard erect a pair of brackets on either side of the centreline, so that the space between each pair will be a push-fit for the keel, the forward pair being so placed that when the keel is in position on the board, they will just grip the outer end of the stemhead, while the after pair should be just clear of the counter, *Sketch No.* 17. I have found metal shelf brackets do this job very well, but it is advisable to check them to make certain that they are really square, for such brackets are not always dead-true, and if there is any doubt it is better to make two pairs of hardwood brackets, since on these will depend the truth of the model. As will be obvious from the sketches, the height of these brackets will have to be such as to reach the stemhead forward, and project above the level of the counter aft.

In assembling the keel and stem and stern-posts we have left an extension both fore and aft, and these drop down between the pairs of brackets at bow and stern respectively. The forward pair also grip the stemhead, while the upper ends of the after pair register on a temporary spar attached to the stern-post and transom. *Sketch No.* 17. In this way the stem and stern-post are kept truly perpendicular throughout the entire construction period, and twisting out of shape is impossible, yet the model can be lifted right out of the building jig at any time for inspection, admiration (the most common reason!), or work, and instantly replaced when no longer required. It is the most satisfactory form of building jig I have so far discovered, far in advance of the more common arrangement of a ridge spar and struts, since it leaves the whole model readily accessible, both inside and out, while the fact that one can lift the hull completely out of the jig at any time, and at any stage of construction, often simplifies work in difficult corners.

The keel assembly will now be dry and fit to handle, so from the constructional plan or sheer-plan, cut cardboard templates of the shapes of both stem and stern-posts, including a length of the keel in both, so that the true angles of these posts can be fixed. Lay the template of the stem on the "rough", and having made certain that the base is true to the keel, run a pencil round it to mark the finished shape of the stem on the "rough", after which it can be sawn out, but remember not to cut off the portion of the keel which extends forward of the stem. *Sketch No.* 14. Treat the stern-post in the same way. By making all the joints in the keel assembly while the stem and stern-posts are in the rough, you will have ensured that as finally cut out these members are in true relation to the keel, and that any slight error in making the joints will not have effected the finished job. Had the components been first finished and then joined together, any error in the joints of the stem for example, would have thrown out the angle of the upper face of the stemhead, and with it the steeve of the bowsprit.

When the keel assembly is finished, clean off the paper which will have stuck to it in jointing, then lay it on the building plan and carefully mark in all the station lines for the frames, after which it should be placed in the jig, the midship frame centred over the midship frame drawn on the base, and while in position, pin down a small block of wood at either end of the keel, so that whenever the model is removed and replaced, it will always go back with the frames correctly located in relation to the base-board, and the jig is now complete.

I have referred to dowelled joints, so perhaps this would be a good place to describe the making of dowelling suitable for this purpose. Thin dowelling may be made from either boxwood or bamboo, but personally I favour the latter, since not only is it stronger size for size, but also bamboo can first be split down to the approximate size, whereas boxwood has to be sawn down. Of course if your model is being built in boxwood, then the use of the same material for the dowels will mean that they are slightly less noticeable in the finished product, but I do not think this is really so very important in most cases, while if the model is to be painted or stained, then there is no advantage at all.

I always use bamboo, and some twenty odd years ago I bought an old tripod flower-pot stand which cost me a few coppers in a "junk" shop, and not only has it supplied all the material I have needed since that time, but would last as long again, should I be in a position to require it! This stand was made of bamboo about $1\frac{1}{2}$" diameter, and stuff of this size or larger is the best for making dowels, since the distance between knuckles is greater than in the smaller diameter material, while the fact of the walls being thicker means that several lengths of dowelling can be made from each piece split off. Dowelling can best be made by using a draw-plate as shown in *Sketch No.* 18. This consists of a steel plate about 3/32 ins. thick, through which a range of holes, decreasing in size, is drilled, all holes being counter-sunk on one side as shown in the section. I have two plates, each with 20 holes, giving a complete range of sizes from a No. 40 down to a No. 80 drill, but for many years I used to make draw-plates as I needed them, from bits of old "hoop-iron", such as is used round casks and barrels, and they worked quite well. Of course they did not last very long because they would not keep a cutting edge, but when that happened I simply drilled another set of holes and started again. A pair of good steel draw-plates are of course the best, but the fact that the reader does not have such a thing need not prevent him from making dowels.

The process of making dowelling is very simple, and clearly shown in *Sketch No.* 19. Split down a length of bamboo—or saw out a strip of box-

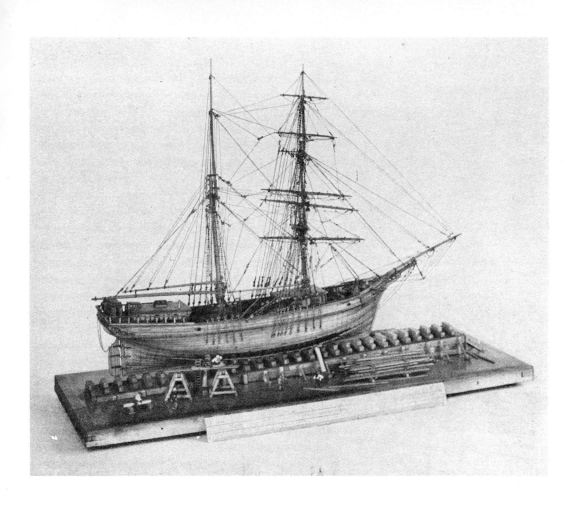

Fig. 1.
THE BRIGANTINE *LEON*
1/8 in. Scale Model by the Author.
(Shipyard workers repairing planking).

Fig. 2.
THE BRIGANTINE *LEON*
The Author's 1/8 in. Scale Model, Port Side
(Rigging still to "cleaned up").

wood—to about twice the diameter of the required dowelling. Hold the draw-plate in the vice, or by hand if a vice is not handy, and having sharpened the end of the bamboo, pass it through one of the larger holes from the opposite side to the counter-sink; grip the point in a pair of flat nosed pliers, give a sharp pull, and the strip will come out with the corners taken off. Repeat the process using a smaller hole each time, until you reach the size of drill for which the dowelling is required on the job in hand. In my model of *Leon* I used about No. 52 drill for the heavy work in the frame construction, No. 57 for the plank and deck fixings, and down as low as No. 75 for such things as the panels of the deckhouses. To see this very fine dowelling when made, as thin as very fine cotton, it looks too frail to be of any use whatever, yet if made from bamboo it is surprisingly strong for its size, and quite strong enough for fixing small rails, panels and the like. This to me is very important, for as I will explain later, I never leave *anything* to adhesive, but every single item, no matter how small, is always pinned or dowelled. That is one of my pet obsessions.

The lengths of dowelling made should be the maximum the spacing between knuckles in the bamboo used will allow, or about six or nine inches in the case of boxwood. In use I usually slightly point or round one end of a length of dowelling by rubbing it on a piece of very fine sandpaper, then dip that end in knotting, or failing that very thin glue, and push it as far into the hole as it will go by hand, then break it off, leaving enough projecting from the hole to allow it to be diriven as far as necessary, with a very light hammer. I made my dowelling hammer from a piece of 3/8 in. square bar about 1¼ in. long, fitted on a piece of steel wire, with a small file handle as a grip. This turned out a very nice tool to use for this job, just about the right weight and balance. The head of the dowel will be cleaned up when work gets its final dressing with sandpaper or a very fine file.

One great advantage of using bamboo or wood dowels instead of metal fixings is that no harm is done if, where long fixings have to be driven at different angles, one should run into another at some point, also the dowel, when touched with knotting before driving, becomes part of the wood into which it is driven, and not a foreign body as in the case of metal fixings. Another important point, particularly in making frames, is that a joint can be dowelled before the final cutting to shape, as in *Sketches No. 14 and No.* 27 and then sawn out leaving the dowels intact and without any damage to the saw.

The next job will be to build up the deadwood at bow and stern, *Sketches No. 9 and* 10. The deadwood serves the dual purpose of strengthening the stem and stern-post respectively, and also forming a sound landing for both frames and planking at points where the hull is particularly narrow. In a small model this deadwood can be cut out in the form of solid knees as shown in the constructional plan *Plate No.* 2, but I avoid all heavy work as far as possible and enjoy assembling small components, so I built it up of small pieces of 1/4 in. square material. First make a rough tracing of the complete keel, stem, stern-post and deadwood from the construction plan, and pin this down on a board, then remove the keel assembly from the building jig and lay it in position on this tracing, fixing it either with panel pins driven round it at points clear of the deadwood fore and aft, or as I usually do, lightly glue it down to the paper. Then with the tracing below as a guide cut and glue in position the knees which are to be used as deadwood, or alternatively build up the deadwood as I did from small pieces of 1/4 in. square hardwood, cutting and glueing down each piece in turn until the required shape and area is covered. When the deadwood is in position, whether made from the solid or built up, cover it with a piece of paper and lay a flat-iron on top until the glue has had time to set. In the case of the built-up method it is a matter of choice whether you lay the sections in straight horizontal members, straight diagonal members as in the stern of the American barquentine *Newsboy*, *Sketch No*. 10, or in a radial form as with the British ship in *Sketch No*. 9.

When the glue has had time to dry, dowel through both keel, stem and stern-posts respectively, into the deadwood, while in the case of the built-up job, also dowel down from the inside so that every component will be reached. After this clean off any paper sticking to the assembly, and rule the frame lines, already shown on the keel, stem and stern-post, across the deadwood on both sides. While doing this also add the water lines, measured from the Sheer-plan, for you will require these for the next operation, marking out the bearding line and rabbet.

The outer edge of the rabbet for the planking, or rabbet-line as it is termed, is always shown on the profile drawing since this represents the end of the planking as seen in the finished ship, while a constructional plan, such as that produced here as *Plate No*. 2, will also contain the inner one called the bearding-line, but when this is not shown on the plans it will have to be worked out by the builder. This however is not as difficult as it may sound, and as soon as the basic principle is understood it will prove an exceedingly simple process, in fact it is far more difficult to explain than to carry out. The first thing is to discover whether the Lines Plan has been drawn to the inside or outside of the planking. In almost all builders' plans for merchant ships, both large and small, the Lines will be to the inside of the planking since that is the most suitable arrangement for setting out the frames etc., but in most plans drawn for models the Lines will be to the outside of the planking, because that gives the true external shape of the hull and is suitable for building either solid block or laminated models. However, but for one slight variation, the method of setting out the rabbet for the planking is the same in either case, and that variation will be covered as we go along.

We will assume that the builder has to work from an ordinary set of model plans and that the Lines are drawn to the outside of the planking. On both sides of the model stem and stern-post set out the rabbet-line ("R" in *Sketch No. 20B*) which will be shown in both proflle and Lines Drawing of your set of plans. Then on the Half-breadth Plan—the one showing the shapes of the various waterlines—draw *inside* each waterline at both bow and stern, the thickness of planking to be used, as shown by the dotted lines in *Sketch No. 20A*. (In this sketch each waterline has been treated separately for the sake of clarity in showing the shape of the rabbet at the various levels). Now with your compasses measure *along the face* of the stern-post in the Half-breadth Plan, the distance between the inner and outer faces of the planking at the highest waterline, as "a" on W.L.5 in *Sketch No. 20A*. Transfer this to the same waterline pencilled on the stern-post, as shown in *Sketch No. 20B*, marking it on both sides of the wood. Repeat this for each waterline in turn, then run a line through each of the dots so found, and you will have the inner edge of the rabbet complete as shown in the last sketch referred to. The bottom part of this line will of course run out over the deadwood, but that is one of the reasons why the deadwood is there. The rabbet should now be cut between these two lines, and its shape at the various levels will appear something like those shown in the *Sketch No. 20A*. Set out the rabbet of the stem in the same way, followed by that of the keel, for which the thickness of the planking is set off inside the station lines in the Body Plan and set out vertically instead of horizontally.

If you are working from an original shipyard plan, which is not very probable since very few of these old wooden ships were built from plans, the normal method being to set out the lines full size from a half-model after the latter had been shaped "by eye" to what the builder required. However if you should have such a plan, the bearding line will probably be shown, as well as the rabbet line, but if these are to be of any use you will have to use scale thickness planking, otherwise it will still be necessary to set out the bearding line to suit the material you intend to use. Of course if you have a full construction plan to the scale of the model, such as that reproduced as *Plate No. 2* no setting out will be required.

The next stage will be to build the framing of the counter, and in the plans I have shown this in a simplified form, using a fashion-piece as is common practice in model yacht construction, but in my own model I framed the counter, since this not only offered a more interesting form of construction, but also cut out any form of carving from the solid, which both resembled work, and would in any case not have been suitable for my card-table workshop. Professor Favez whose model has been used to illustrate this book, also followed this construction from sketches of the method used when I built mine. However I will deal with both methods,

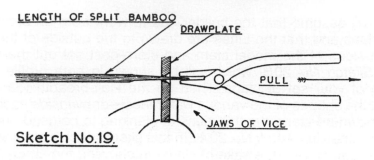

LENGTH OF SPLIT BAMBOO

DRAWPLATE

PULL →

JAWS OF VICE

Sketch No.19.

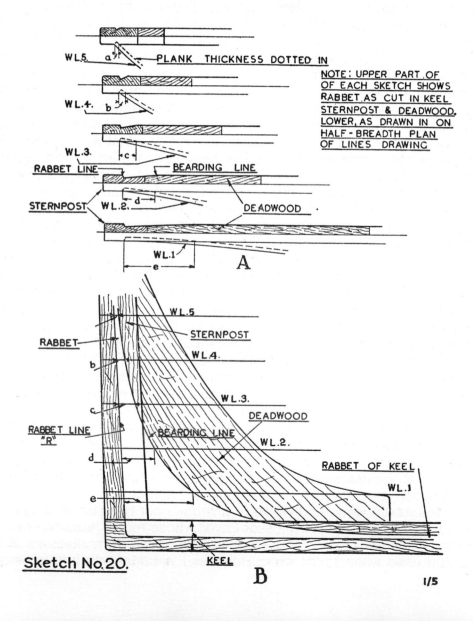

WL.5.   a   PLANK THICKNESS DOTTED IN

WL.4.   b

WL.3.

RABBET LINE   BEARDING LINE

STERNPOST   WL.2.   d   DEADWOOD

WL.1

e

A

NOTE: UPPER PART OF
OF EACH SKETCH SHOWS
RABBET AS CUT IN KEEL
STERNPOST & DEADWOOD,
LOWER, AS DRAWN IN ON
HALF-BREADTH PLAN
OF LINES DRAWING

WL.5

RABBET   STERNPOST

b   WL.4.

WL.3.

c   DEADWOOD

RABBET LINE
"R"   BEARDING LINE   WL.2.

d   RABBET OF KEEL

WL.1

e

Sketch No.20.

KEEL

B

although I strongly advocate the latter

If the simplified method is used, then the first job is to fit the horn-timbers *Plate No.* 2. These are two strips of 3/16 in x 1/8 in. hardwood dowelled on either side of the stern-post as shown in the constructional plan referred to, with their outer ends morticed into the fashion-piece as indicated. The fashion-piece should be carved from the solid, using the full size detail included on the drawing. When the carving is complete fit a small bracket inside between the mortices for the horn-timbers, and extending just far enough forward to leave sufficient clearance for the rudder stock to pass between it and the stern-post, in fact this bracket forms the after side of the rudder-trunk. On top of the bracket and fashion-piece screw a piece of hardwood, having the same thickness as the keel and projecting an inch or so over the stern, as in *Sketch No.* 21. Take great care in fixing this temporary spar to ensure that it is dead over the centreline and runs truly parallel to the keel, since its object is to engage between the after pair of brackets of the building jig, and on it will depend the truth of the hull. Another method would be to use a single spar running the length of the ship, over both stem and stern, just as the keel does below, but there are several objections to this, such as the difference in angles of the tops of stem and fashion-piece, and above all the obstruction it would offer when fitting bilge-stringers, deckbeams, etc., so I prefer the two short members, providing that they are carefully fixed.

When the fashion-piece is finished fit it on to the horn-timbers, but without glue, and put the whole assembly into the building jig. Carefully check the fashion-piece for being square with the centreline of the ship, and also measure up from the base to each corner in turn to verify that it is perfectly horizontal thwartships. When satisfied, apply some thin glue to the mortices and the ends of the horn-timbers, replace the fashion-piece, then put the whole assembly back into the jig for a final check up before the glue has time to set, then when quite satisfied, leave to get hard. If your mortices for the horn-timbers have been properly cut there will be no trouble about assembling this stern frame, but if desired the horn-timbers could be clamped in position on the stern-post during the early stages of fitting instead of being glued and dowelled, but this could be only a temporary measure, for they must be glued and dowelled before finally fitting the fashion-piece since they are its only means of support at this stage. When the glue in the mortices is dry, the horn-timbers should then be dowelled to the sides of the bracket projecting inboard from the fashion-piece.

I will now deal with the built-up stern as illustrated by Professor Favez's model and the wash drawings, *Fig.* 6 *and* 13. In place of the normal frame at station No. 22^1/$_2$ *Plate No.* 2 a solid bulkhead as in *Sketch No.* 22 is fitted astride the deadwood. Then a series of laminations—an

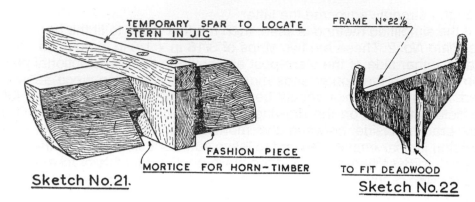

TEMPORARY SPAR TO LOCATE
STERN IN JIG

FRAME Nº 22½

FASHION PIECE
MORTICE FOR HORN—TIMBER

TO FIT DEADWOOD

Sketch No. 21.

Sketch No. 22

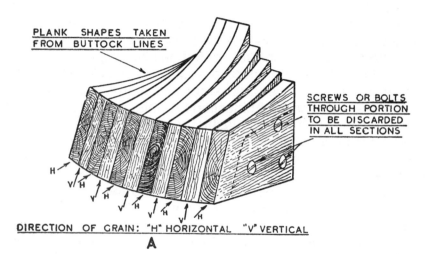

PLANK SHAPES TAKEN
FROM BUTTOCK LINES

SCREWS OR BOLTS
THROUGH PORTION
TO BE DISCARDED
IN ALL SECTIONS

H

V H V H V H V H

DIRECTION OF GRAIN: "H" HORIZONTAL "V" VERTICAL

A

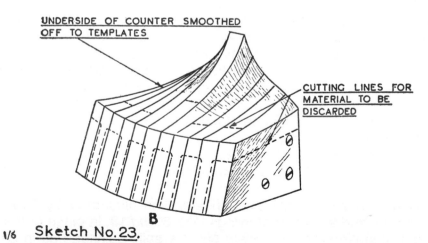

UNDERSIDE OF COUNTER SMOOTHED
OFF TO TEMPLATES

CUTTING LINES FOR
MATERIAL TO BE
DISCARDED

B

1/6 Sketch No. 23.

odd number—are marked out based on the buttock lines, to which they are roughly cut and then screwed together, the screws being placed in that part of the material which will be cut away and discarded when the frame is finished. In arranging the laminations the centre one must have the grain running vertically, while those on either side are placed with the grain alternatively horizontal and vertical—*Sketch No. 23A*—the reason for which will be seen later. When the laminations are screwed together the whole is shaped up to form a solid counter, using cross templates and templates of the buttock lines, just as in building a normal laminated hull. *Sketch No. 23B.* When the shaping is complete the laminations are taken apart for the removal of the unwanted sections, discarding in each case the lower portions of those in which the grain runs vertically, and the upper parts of those with horizontal grain. To facilitate accurate re-assembly the templates used for shaping should be retained, and when the unwanted portions, as indicated in the sketches, have been cut away, the whole frame is carefully rebuilt by glueing and dowelling each member, working outward from the centre, and constantly checking with the templates as the work proceeds. When finished the complete unit will look as in *Sketch No. 24.* The thinning down of the stanchions and the fitting of the side frames is all done after the main construction has been glued and dowelled. With this construction the first lamination on either side of the central one takes the place of the horn-timbers, while the longer extension on the base of the central stanchion forms the after end of the rudder-trunk, as did the bracket fitted on the inside of the fashion-piece in the case of the alternative construction. The form of fabricated stern frame just described, provides a perfect landing for the planks under the counter and across the transom, as well as providing a bit of interesting construction work which is devoid of any hard labour, which is to me far preferable to carving a fashion-piece from the solid. In fixing, the ends of the horizontal members are glued to the face of the solid frame No. 23, and afterwards dowelled, while the members forming the horn-timbers are glued to both solid frame and the stern-post, and of course dowelled to the former; all this being done as the stern frame is being assembled, so that the stern-post and solid frame help to support each member as it goes into place. The whole backbone of the model now being complete the temporary spar from the stern-post and projecting aft over the centre stanchion of the stern-frame *Top Sketch No. 24* can be fitted and the model returned to the jig, where it will appear as in *Sketch No. 17*, and left while we consider the construction of the frames.

The general construction of full-size frames will be clear from *Sketch No. 25.* This actually shows frames built in pairs, but the fabrication of each unit remains the same whether built singly or in pairs. Each frame is made up of a number of sections known as "floors", "futtocks" and "top

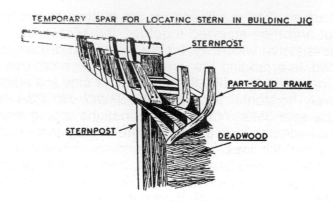

TEMPORARY SPAR FOR LOCATING STERN IN BUILDING JIG

STERNPOST

PART-SOLID FRAME

STERNPOST

DEADWOOD

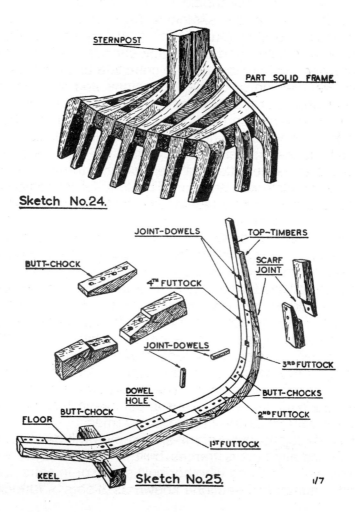

STERNPOST

PART SOLID FRAME

Sketch No.24.

JOINT-DOWELS   TOP-TIMBERS

BUTT-CHOCK   SCARF
                    JOINT

4TH FUTTOCK

3RD FUTTOCK

JOINT-DOWELS

DOWEL   BUTT-CHOCKS
HOLE

FLOOR   BUTT-CHOCK   2ND FUTTOCK

KEEL   Sketch No.25.   1ST FUTTOCK

1/7

timbers", respectively. The floor is that part of the frame which extends right across the keel, joining the two halves on either side of the ship, while the futtocks are any sections which do not go right across the keel, but make up the sides of the frame. The top-timbers, which may or may not continue right up to the rail and so form the bulwark stanchions, are usually kept relatively short, so that in event of the ship's bulwarks or top-sides being damaged as the result of the rigging carrying away or heavy seas, the top portions of the frames can be replaced without having to strip off too much of the side planking to get at the first joint. Even when the frames do not continue on to form the bulwark stanchions, and this was perhaps, the most common arrangement, the top-timbers were as a rule still kept fairly short, for if a vessel should receive any superficial damage it was usually in the neighbourhood of the deck line, so the advantage of having a joint in the frames somewhere near this level still applied.

In most ships the frames finished at the level of the covering-board of which more later, into which the bulwark stanchions were inserted as separate units, but in small scale model work there is something to be said for making the stanchions at bow and stern as part of the frame, even if inset stanchions are used in the body of the ship This is not a matter of strength, for inserted stanchions can be made equally strong, but of preserving the true sweep of the hull round the flair of the bows and the knuckle of the stern, since it is much easier to work these curves into the end of a continuous frame than to make short separate stanchions fair up properly after being inserted into the hull. However it is a matter of taste, and in a larger model there is little difficulty. If the stanchions are formed as part of the frame, the top of the frame must of course be reduced accordingly.

There were various methods by means of which the futtocks of a frame were joined one to another, but perhaps the most common was that shown in *Sketch No.* 25, where the floors and lower futtocks are linked by means of butt-chocks connecting half-scarf ends on adjoining components. The top-timbers however were almost invariably joined by means of a simple scarf, since this rendered easy their replacement in event of damage. Sometimes frames were scarfed throughout, but in that case the lower joints would be made with a full scarf as in *Sketch No. 26A*, while another method was the square-butt joint, with a central dowel as *No. 26B*. So it will be seen that unless the model builder has the actual constructional details of the ship he is reproducing, he has several alternatives in full-size practice to choose from, to say nothing of the purely model styles which bear no resemblance to the real thing, such as the full bulkhead, the "one-piece" frame, neither of which appeal to me, or the bent frame.

The main reason for the many segments in the full-size frame was of

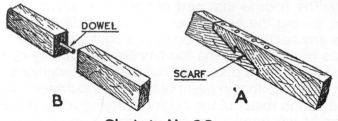

DOWEL

SCARF

B   'A'

Sketch No.26.

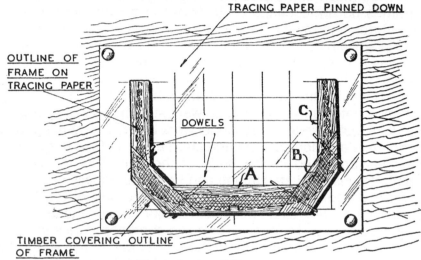

TRACING PAPER PINNED DOWN

OUTLINE OF
FRAME ON
TRACING PAPER

C

DOWELS

B

A

TIMBER COVERING OUTLINE
OF FRAME

Sketch No.27.

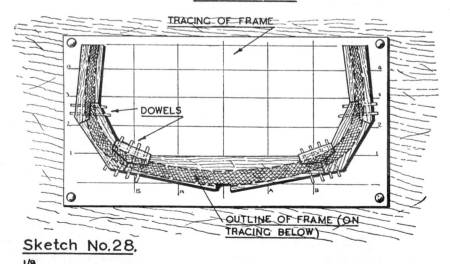

TRACING OF FRAME

DOWELS

OUTLINE OF FRAME (ON
TRACING BELOW)

Sketch No.28.

1/8

course the need to take the grain round the curves, and in a well built ship the grain really *did* go all round the curve, which is something I would like to carry out in a model some day, just for the pleasure of doing it. In model work the grain rarely really follows the sweep of the curve all the way, but is made of a series of more or less straight-grained sections which, by being joined together, take the grain round the frame as a whole, but not round the individual curves. The old wooden-ship building yard usually carried a good stock of well seasoned timber of suitable thickness for frame making and selected for its wavy grain, and as the frames were being built, the templates, or moulds, were laid out on the various bulks and each piece selected so that the natural grain followed as closely as possible the curve of that particular futtock. This selection of timber to suit the particular bend required also had something to do with the placing of the joints, although care was always taken to avoid joints in adjoining frames falling in a direct line.

Now to return to the model. The plans show the square-butt and central dowel type of construction, but the reader can make his own choice, it will make no difference to the construction of the model as a whole, and for the purpose of this description I think we will take the most simple form, the plain scarfed joint as in *Sketch No.* 27, but should the butt-chock joint, with proper scarfs for the top-timbers be preferred, the method of making the frames will be the same, except that there will be a few more joints to make in the "rough", but as these are all to be made before shaping, *Sketch No. 28*, no difficulties will be experienced. The *Leon* model has single frames. but even though the reader should desire to build a model with double frames, the general principle will be the same and I will deal with the minor details later. The construction of a double frame can be the most simple of all, even more so than the type now to be described.

The method of transferring the frame shape to paper has already been covered, so we will assume that the builder has now made an outline drawing of the midship frame. This should be done on tracing paper since it is important for this method of construction that it should be readable from both sides. Next add the internal shape of the frame, as shown on the constructional plan *Plate No. 2*. Where no such drawing is available the builder will have to settle on the moulded size he intends to use at various points round the frame, and draw the internal cutting line accordingly. Do not be tempted to draw this internal shape carelessly, but having decided on the scantlings see that they are repeated in all other frames so that the keelson, bilge-stringers, deck-beam-shelves and internal rails will run smoothly on the inner faces of all frames, this is most important, for if they will not rest properly on the frames you will land in a lot of trouble at a later stage. This is just another example of the point I have tried to make in Chapter I., that plank-on-frame construction is not really difficult providing proper attention is paid to detail when making the various components which go to form the whole.

There is no bevel on the midship frame, so that is a matter which need not bother us at the moment, and having made your drawing, not forgetting the levels of the deck, rail and wale, for you will want these on your frame later, pin it on a flat surface, *pencil side down*, making certain that the paper is stretched flat. Now take a length of the material to be used and lay it across the drawing so it just covers the lower section of the frame (the floor), as seen through the tracing paper *"A" Sketch No.* 27. Mark the ends so that they will form a simple scarf, or angular joint, just where the frame starts to change direction, and cut them off. Now lay other pieces against these so that they cover the next section of the frame *B*, cutting them to the required sizes, followed by the last two pieces *C* made in the same way. Lay them down on the tracing again, carefully fitting each joint so that you get perfect contact throughout, and when satisfied with the joints, and having checked that the drawing of the frame does not show outside the timber at any point, glue them down to the tracing and to each other, taking particular care that the joints are making good contact. When all are in place, cover the "rough" of the frame with a sheet of paper and place a heavy weight on top to ensure that the frame will be perfectly flat when the glue has dried.

This particular sketch shows a typical arrangement of the sections forming a frame of this shape, but of course it is not the only possible layout, and the reader may decide to place his joints and components differently. Only two points are important, first that the grain shall be carried round the frame as far as possible, which in a larger model would mean that there would require to be more futtocks round the turn of the bilge, and secondly that the joints are so arranged that they make an angle which can be through-dowelled. This incidentally is one of the advantages of the butt chock type of joint, there never is any difficulty in getting at the dowels, since there is more room for them to run square across the frame, which is not always the case with a simple angular joint. As the frames change in shape along the hull, so will the arrangement and number of futtocks differ, and before making each frame the builder should try various layouts until he finds the most suitable for the frame in question. The best way to make these experiments is to cut a few strips of card, representing pieces of the material from which the frames are being made, and arrange these round the frame in various combinations, allowing them to overlap at the joints until you arrive at the layout most satisfactory in both run of grain and jointing.

When the glue on the "rough" of a frame has had time to dry, cut away all the paper from round the edges, but still leaving the actual drawing stuck to one side of the timber, since this is the template to which the final

Fig. 3.
A GROUP OF THE AUTHOR'S MODELS
(Showing Scadinavian barque referred to in text)

Fig. 4.
COMBINATION OF "BUILT" AND BENT FRAMES IN MODEL
BY THE AUTHOR (Built-frames in pairs)

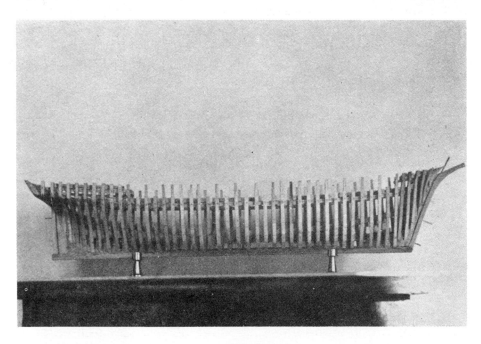

Fig. 5.
READY FOR PLANKING-BATTENS
1/8 in. Scale Model of *LEON* by Professor Favez, Switzerland

cutting will be done. Having got rid of the surplus paper, mark the run of the dowels, taking care that they will pass through the centre of the joint *inside* the finished frame. Drill the holes and drive home the dowels, which will of course have been dipped in knotting as already mentioned. All that now remains to be done is to cut out the frame to the outline shown on the tracing which is stuck to it, clean up the inboard and outboard faces and transfer to these the lines representing the rail and deck or wale, after which the fore and aft sides can be rubbed down to remove all traces of paper adhering to them. The fore and aft faces can now be either varnished or French polished according to whether they are to be exposed or covered, and the frame laid aside for this to dry. The face which is to receive the planking will of course be left bare, as will be the inner face until the bilge-stringers and deck-shelves have been fitted. The mortice which saddles the keel will of course have been cut out with the frame, but I think it better to leave this just a shade small at the original cutting, so that it can be finally fitted to the keel, doing the final dressing with a fine warding file. This must be a good fit on the keel, not only as a tight joint, but also so that the frame sits both square thwartships, and true in the vertical too. The depth of the mortice is such that the edge of the frame lines up with the inner edge of the rabbet of the keel, while the depth of material above the keel must of course be the same in all frames if the keelson is to sit properly and also lock the frames in position as it should.

I have always found that a good cold adhesive is the best for this part of the work, for with certain tracing papers hot glue makes them contract, which can throw the frame a little out of truth, although if the glue is applied quickly and the frame got under weights immediately this is not likely to happen. However it is better to use a cold adhesive and so avoid all such risk. Another safeguard is to use a good heavy tracing paper, say 90 or 110 grm. weight. This is perfectly transparent, yet has sufficient body not to be effected by the adhesive. Alternatively, you can make a rubbing of your drawing before you pin it down, and mark your frame from a template instead of cutting to the line on the paper. To make this rubbing, lay your drawing face down on a piece of white card, then with a sharp pencil go over the lines seen through the paper, which when removed will have left a copy on the card. The "rough" can then be built on the original drawing and the card cut out to form a template from which the finished shape of the frame is marked. However I have never found this necessary, but have always used the drawing stuck to the wood.

All frames both fore and aft of midships will have to be bevelled to the run of the hull, and the further forward or aft you go, the more bevel there will be on the frame, further, this bevel will differ in different parts of the same frame. You can of course make all your frames square on the edge and cut the bevel afterwards, when they are in the hull, but this is not so simple as it sounds. In the first place the bevel must be cut before the wale goes on, and in this state the frames are largely unsupported, so there is a risk of racking them out of position, to say nothing of the possibility of damage to the edges. Personally I think it always pays to put the bevel on the frames while they are still on the bench, to set it out properly from the drawings and not leave it to be found by trial and error and the use of battens. If you cut the bevel while the frame is on the bench you will know that when it comes to planking, every plank will sit properly on every frame, which is what you want. In any case there is no difficulty in putting the correct bevel on the frames before they go into the ship, it is set out exactly as are the frames themselves.

On your Lines Plan you have already ruled two lines for each frame, one, that nearest the midship frame, representing the frame station, and the other the forward or after edge according to whether the frame is in the fore or after body. When lifting off the shape of the frame you will have worked from the face nearest to the midship line, since that is the frame station, but having set out this shape on the paper from which the frame is to be made, do the same for the line representing the face of the frame away from the midship frame, and set this out on the same drawing, so that you now have two outlines, one of which will run slightly inside the other. In other words, you treat the fore and aft edges of the frame as two separate frames but set them down on one sheet of paper, as shown by the full and dotted lines in *Sketch No. 29A*. Having completed the outlines of your "two frames", proceed to draw in the inside shape of each as shown in the sketch, and the difference between the full and dotted line in each case represents the varying degrees of taper on the different parts of the frame. In sawing out the frame, the outside edge is cut to the full line, and the inside shape to the dotted line, after which the frame is bevelled back to the inner line in each case, not forgetting of course that the bevel runs in the same direction on both inboard and outboard faces, as shown in the Sketch 29*B*.

The bevel on the inboard face is every bit as important as that on the other, for if it is not carefully cut, your bilge-stringers and deck-shelves will not run properly. This matter of setting the bevels down on paper is another of those things which sound very complicated, but which in practice offer no difficulty whatever. If you can set out the main shape of the frame then you can set out the bevel, for all it means is that you set out both sides of the frame on one sheet of paper, and the difference between them is the bevel. It is as simple as that. One last point and we will move on. If you are making the bulwark stanchions as part of the frames, do not forget to reduce them to a suitable thickness above the covering-board, remember also that not every frame will form a stanchion, for the latter are much more widely spread, except perhaps in way of the rigging in cases where this is set up on the rail and not on the deck or outside channels.

The midship frame is now ready for fixing, so there is no reason why it should not go into place. The keel, stem and stern-frame assembly are complete and in the building jig, and now that we are about to start framing, should not be taken out again until all square frames are in position, or better still, until all the frames are in and the whole tied together by means of wales, keelson, bilge-stringers and deck-shelves, but in actual fact it may prove an advantage to take the model out when fixing the cant-frames, but we will see. When once the frames are tied together you can take the model out as often as you like, and in the later stages most of the actual work will be done outside the jig, which is then largely used to prevent the ship pulling out of shape if, for example, you have to leave it with one side rather further advanced than the other.

In full-size practice as each frame is installed it would be shored and braced from the building berth, a ridge-spar, and any other fixed object which would stiffen it, to say nothing of temporary battens running round the hull as soon as one or two frames were in place, but in this matter of fixing frames I cheat a little by using a jig which can be put in place when required and removed at will, as for example when sitting to admire the little ship taking shape! This jig is shown in *Sketch No.* 30 and consists of a piece of thin plywood—for my last model I found a bit of "hard-board" which served perfectly—stiffened by a rail of 1/2" or 3/4" stuff screwed on the underside to prevent sagging.

On this board draw in the centreline and then notch the ends to be a good fit round the stem and stern posts respectively. The fitting of these notches is important, in fact the most important part of the jig, for they must be so made that when lowered into position the jig always comes to rest at the level of the highest waterline on the Lines Drawing. When the end notches are correct, square up from the baseboard the position of the midship frame, marking on both edges of the jig and ruling the line right across. Mark in all the other frames, either the same way or by setting off by direct measurement on the jig. Next set out the outline of the hull at the level of the waterline at which the jig sits, as taken from the Half-breadth Plan, after which the jig can be cut out, leaving this line just showing. If your Lines Plan has been drawn to the outside of the planking, as in most model plans, then another line representing the thickness of the planking must be run inside the first one, and this line will be the outer face of each frame at the level of the jig. Finally draw in the sided thickness of the frames and cut notches in the sides of the jig. These notches should be a nice fit on the frames in a fore-and-aft direction, but a little deeper than the moulded dimension at that point, just to allow a little freedom for the final fitting of the frame to the keel. The purpose of this jig will be obvious, it sits, when required, like a level deck on which is located the exact width of every frame at that level; it supplies a fixed centreline when needed, much better than the usual thread stretched from stem to stern-post, and at the same time it ensures that every frame is truly perpendicular to the keel, in fact it provides an immediate three-dimensional check on each frame as it goes in. Taking the model as a whole this jig saves hours of not very interesting work in squaring up each frame by means of a steel square from the base, first one side and then the other, as well as the thwartship checking, by measurement either from a stretched centreline or from the base. It also acts as a jig to hold the frame in position until the glue in the joint with the keel has time to set, while at a later stage it will be used to support the frames during the fitting of the heavy wale round the hull, so time spent making an accurate job of this jig is not only time well spent, but also much time saved.

Now take up the finished midship frame, in which the mortice requires the final fitting. Offer it to the keel at the point where the latter is marked for the midship frame and open it up with a fine warding file until it sits properly, checking the top of the frame with the jig. When the mortice is a good fit, give it a touch of glue and replace it in position, put on the jig to check and hold the frame until the glue sets.

By the time you have the next frame ready the model will be fit to handle again, in fact when once you get into the way of working you will probably have two frames in hand at the same time, one with the "rough" under weights until dry, while the second is being set out on paper ready for glueing up, then while the glue in this is drying you will go back to the other and get it cut out and fitted. Continue making and fitting the frames in this way until you reach the points at either end where they no longer sit on the keel, but have to be fixed to the deadwood, which in *Leon* is frame 4½ forward and 19½ aft, the last square frame in each case being Nos. 5 and 19 respectively.

Before going any further the keelson should be fitted, which will firmly lock the frames which are already in place. In the deadwood at either end a step will have been left to receive the ends of the keelson, the rise of these steps being the same as the thickness of the frames above the top of the keel, so that when the keelson is laid in place it will rest both on the steps and also along the top of the frames. In this model a single keelson is fitted, which is sufficiently strong for the model, although in full-size practice it would probably carry a rider-keelson on top, while in large wooden ships two or three rider-keelsons might well be fitted. In wood-built ships it is of course the keelsons and not the keel which form the real backbone of the vessel, and in some of the very large wooden ships built in America, the keelsons were built up to a depth of five or six feet of solid timber, as well as being placed three abreast along the top of the frames. Another source of strength was the ceiling, or inner lining. The ceiling in a ship has nothing in common with its namesake ashore, for it actually forms the bottom of the hold, but is also carried right up the sides too, in fact it is a complete inner skin of planking, laid just like the outer skin, but usually very much thicker on either side of the keelson, tapering in thickness as it reaches the turn of the bilge. In a large ship it may be made up of 12 in. x 12 in. timbers at the keelson, reducing to about 6 in. thick in the sides of the ship. Thick belts were also run immediately below the beam-shelves of each deck, and these provided much of the longitudinal strength of the ship. In small craft the ceiling sometimes ended at the turn of the bilge, so that it merely formed the floor of the hold, but in larger vessels it carried right round from keelson to the underside of the upper deck, and differed from the external planking only in its thickness and the fact that a strake was omitted here and there to allow ventilation between the frames.

In designing the *Leon* model I had originally intended that it be planked throughout, and therefore did not include either rider-keelson or ceiling, the idea being to produce a model which would provide all the pleasure of "building" a ship on full-size lines, but without putting in all the internal fittings. In a model which is to have most of the planking omitted, or one in which there are large hatches which it is intended to leave open, then these internal details should be included.

We will now assume that in the model being built all the frames from No. 5 to 19 are in position, and before those on either side, i.e. Nos. 4½ and 19½ can be fixed, the keelson must be in place, so that will be the next job. Select a piece of 1/4 in. x 1/4 in. hardwood, and after checking that it is free from twist, cut off a length which will just fit into the steps in the deadwood at either end. This should be a good fit, for the object of the keelson is to tie the two ends of the ship together. Check that it makes good contact with the tops of the frames, or to be correct, the "floors", and if any of them should prove to be a shade out of truth, dress them down until the keelson sits flush fore and aft. See that you have a few lengths of dowelling at hand, together with a drop of knotting in an old tin lid. Dowelling made with a No. 54 drill will be about right for this job, but anything near that will do. Now take a drill of the same size as the dowelling and fit it into a hollow pin-chuck, *Sketch No.* 31, then measure down from the top of the keelson to the baseboard and set the drill to project this distance from the jaws of the chuck as shown. This will allow the holes to be drilled deep enough to just break through the keel without going far enough to fix it to the baseboard, so allowing the dowel to get a good grip. It is always as well to allow a dowel to go right through when possible, since it prevents any risk of forming an air pocket at the bottom of the hole, so perhaps preventing the dowel from getting right home.

Put some glue on the seats for the keelson in the deadwood at either

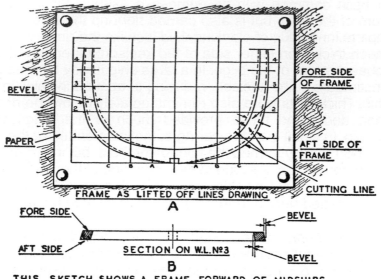

BEVEL

PAPER

FORE SIDE
OF FRAME

AFT SIDE OF
FRAME

CUTTING LINE

FRAME AS LIFTED OFF LINES DRAWING

A

FORE SIDE

AFT SIDE

BEVEL

SECTION ON W.L. Nº 3

BEVEL

B

THIS SKETCH SHOWS A FRAME FORWARD OF MIDSHIPS

Sketch No. 29.

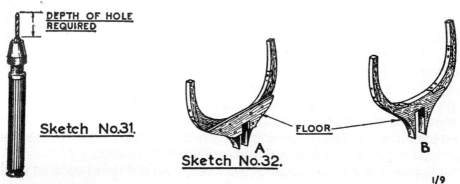

NOTCHES TO LOCATE FRAMES

Sketch No. 30.

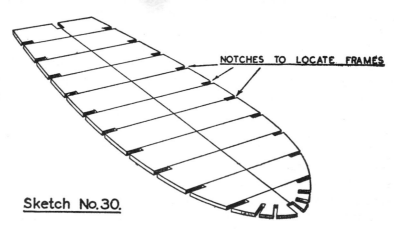

DEPTH OF HOLE
REQUIRED

Sketch No. 31.

FLOOR

A

B

Sketch No. 32.

1/9

end; on top of each frame where the keelson will rest, and also on the ends of the keelson itself. Put the keelson in place and line it up, then starting with the midship frame, drill a hole down through the keelson, frame and keel, until the jaws of the pin-chuck make contact with the wood. Take up a length of dowelling; take the sharp corners off one end by twisting it on a piece of fine sandpaper, dip this end in the knotting, then push it into the hole as far as it will go by hand, cut off some little distance above the surface of the keelson and finish driving with your small dowelling hammer, then when properly home, break or cut off flush with the surface of the wood. For a job such as this where you cannot allow the dowel to come out on the opposite side of the work, it is advisable to mark the dowelling with the length required, then there will be no risk of cutting it off too short, or alternatively driving it so far that you lift the keel off the baseboard. Whenever possible it is advisable to let a dowel go right through the work, afterwards cutting off the surplus from both sides, but in this case this cannot be done, unless of course you remove the model from the building jig for dowelling the frames, in which case there would be no need to measure the length of the drill. Continue dowelling each frame in turn, always working outwards, one forward and one aft, until you reach the ends, when the keelson is dowelled to the steps of the deadwood.

You now have fitted all the frames which sit directly on the keel, and the next few frames at either end will require to be joined over the top of the deadwood, either by making them in two halves and joining them by means of a floor running across them as indicated in the section on the Construction Plan *Plate* 2 and *Sketch No.* 32A, or by incorporating the floor in the frame as in *Sketch No.* 32B, but as the deadwood rises more steeply, so is more of the frame in contact with its surface, and floors become unnecessary, since there is now plenty of room to dowel the frames directly to the face of the deadwood. In *Leon* floors were only fitted to frames 4½, 34½, and forward, and 20, 20½ and 21 aft, but of course this will depend upon the hull form of the particular vessel being built, and can only be settled when the various frames are set out on paper. In setting out the frames which fall on the deadwood, you will of course show the latter on your drawing, and this will show you whether there is sufficient landing for the frame without floors. If it is obvious that you cannot dowel the frame properly owing to the deadwood being too shallow, or the angle of the frame too flat, then a floor must be included, In any case the fitting of the floors will enable you to assemble both parts of the frame and join them together while they are still flat on the drawing, which makes for simplicity in final assembly of the model, and so floors, either as separate units or built into the frames, are advisable so long as the depth of the deadwood will allow them to be used. It is an advantage to fit all frames

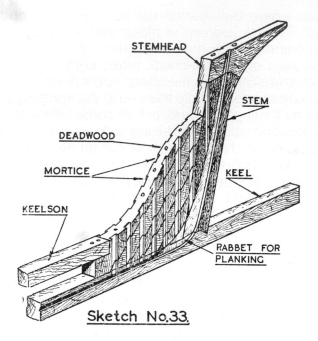

STEMHEAD

STEM

DEADWOOD

MORTICE

KEEL

KEELSON

RABBET FOR PLANKING

Sketch No.33.

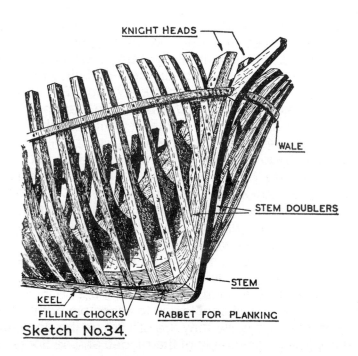

KNIGHT HEADS

WALE

STEM DOUBLERS

STEM

KEEL

FILLING CHOCKS

RABBET FOR PLANKING

Sketch No.34.

on the deadwood in shallow mortices as shown in *Sketch No.* 33, since this not only provides a firmer fixing, but also simplifies the correct location of the frame on the deadwood. When this is done, these mortices should of course be cut at the same time as the rabbet for the planking, i.e. before the stern-frame is fitted and while the stem, keel, and stern-post assembly can be laid flat on the bench, but in setting out your frames, do not forget to allow for the depth of this mortice.

If you have built your stern with the solid fashion-piece instead of the fabricated stern-frame, then all frames from No. 21½ aft, will have to be fitted round the horn-timbers, but with the fabricated stern, the frames run fore-and-aft so this does not arise. At the bow the last square frame in the case of *Leon* is No. 3, forward of which the frames are fitted on the cant. In full size practice filling-chocks were frequently fitted between the stem and the last one or two cant frames, but in *Leon* I merely fitted solid chocks between the stem and the lower parts of the frames, as will be described later. *Sketch No.* 34.

In the Construction Plan for this model I have included full size drawings of the cant-frames, but if the reader is building some other model he will have to lift them off the drawing. However there is no difficulty in this, for when once the frames have been ruled on the Lines Plan, their shape is taken off just as with the square-frames, by measuring out to each waterline in turn, but of course along the angle of the cant. The bevel is also taken off in the same way, by setting out both fore and aft sides of the frame on the same drawing. In fitting, these frames are dowelled to the face of the deadwood, either in mortices or on the flat surface, just as are the square frames, but if they are to be morticed, do not forget to cut the mortices to the angle of the cant. It is very important that the cant-frames be accurately placed, both as to angle and height above the keel, but if you use small cardboard templates for the former and have drawn the waterlines on the frame before cutting out, there is really no difficulty. The templates are used to check that the seat of the frame is cut to the correct angle, and also for a further check when actually fixing, while the level of the frame above the keel is located by lining up the waterlines on the frame with those drawn on the deadwood and stem, just as these waterlines are used for placing the square frames which land on the deadwood.

The next items to go in will be the knightheads, which are two timbers fixed one on either side of the stem-head to confine the bowsprit and receive the ends of the planking on either side of it, see Construction Plan *Plate No.* 2 and *Sketch No.*34. Their after edges butt against the cant-frames "E" (Construction Plan) while their fore edges are bevelled to the run of the planking, a bevel which can be obtained from the run of the rail and deck line in the Lines Drawing. In *Leon* the knightheads are cut off flush with the underside of the rail which, when fixed, will dowel down on

top of them, but in many ships they project well above the rail and termi-
nate either in a carved timber-head, or with their corners chamfered so
that they may be used as temporary bitts to take a turn of rope when
mooring and the like, as shown in the wash-drawings *Fig.* 6 *and* 13. The
knightheads require a little careful fitting, but when once they fit properly
between the first cant-frame and the stem, and are bevelled to the planking, they should be glued and dowelled in position.

The model is now completely framed from stem to stern, and if you
have been careful in cutting your bevels and in setting up the frames, a
thin batten run round the hull in any direction should sit perfectly on them
all, making full contact all the way. There is no reason why you should not
have achieved this, for I think it will be agreed that there has been nothing
really difficult about the work up to date, what your batten test *will* prove,
is whether the work has been carefully done. If you have allowed any
frame to pass which is not quite up to standard, then you will see it now,
but it will be too late to do anything about it. If however you have followed
my original advice and immediately scrapped any frame on which the
chisel has slipped a little too deeply in cutting the bevel, or the saw run a
little too close in cutting out, then your hull will be all right, and you will
have every reason for being glad that you did not decide to "just make it
do".

Right round the outside of the hull at deck level *Leon* has a heavy
wale, 3/32 in. square in the model, but in this she differs from more general practice where the external break in the surface of the planking is
usually well above deck level, however I will say more about that later
when I come to fitting the deck-beams, etc., in the meantime I will deal
with this particular model. This wale serves the dual purpose of binding
the ship together and also acting as a rubbing-belt, but here again there
were several alternatIves, for in many vessels these same objects were
served by providing several strakes of planking, double the normal thickness, in the topsides between the bulwarks and the waterline. However to
return to *Leon*, before starting to fit this wale, see that the top jig is firmly
in position, then make a number of small wedges to fit between the inside
of each of the frames and the bottoms of their respective slots in the jig.
The ideal arrangement would have been to have cut the slots exactly the
depth required in the first place, but there were several objections to this.
For one thing, owing to the tumble-home on the sides midships, the tops
of those frames which also form bulwork stanchions are narrower than at
the level of the jig, and secondly, it is not desirable that the jig should bind
the frame in fitting, since this may have allowed a badly made mortice over
the keel to pass without notice, the jig springing the tops of the frame into
position, only to let them go again when the jig was removed, the object
of the jig at that stage was to check the frames, not to restrain them, at

least as far as thwartships trim was concerned.

The reason for the wedges between the bottoms of the slots and the back of the frames is that at the present stage we do *want* the jig to support them in a thwartship direction during the next operation. There are two alternatives in carrying on the model after all the frames are in, one is to fit the deck-beams before fitting the wale and planking the hull, and the other to leave the beams out altogether until the hull is fully planked, in which case it is as well to provide some support for the tops of the frames while the rather heavy wale is being bent into position, otherwise it might tend to push the frames to one side when the first side was going on. In this model I propose to leave the beams out until after the hull has been planked, since this will give more freedom in getting at the planking, but if we leave out the beams, we must provide something else in their place, and for the purpose of fitting the wale this will be the jig used when framing. When once the wales and bilge-stringers are in, the hull will have ample strength for the rest of the work.

Do not force the wedges in position, they are intended to prevent the frame from moving and not to push it out of truth, they should just fit, and no more. Having made certain that your frames will not move, cut a length of 3/32 in. square material a little longer than is neeessary to go round the outside of the hull. Bevel one end so that it will fit into the rabbet for the planking and will also make good contact with the stem. Put a small piece of wood over this end when it is in position, and with another piece of wood on the opposite side of the stem to protect it, hold the end of the wale in position by means of a clamp or clip. I found that a large size "Bulldog" clip served the purpose quite well. Work the wale round the hull, holding it with small clamps or twisted wire round the frames at intervals as you go. If you find any difficulty in making it run round the hull it can be steamed, but I did not find this necessary, although much will depend upon the type of material being used. Some timber will take the curve better than others, but much can be done by pre-bending before offering it to the hull, either by working it in the hands to something like the curve required, or better still, cut off two suitable lengths of material some time before you are likely to need them, bend them to roughly the shape of the hull and tie their ends with a taut string between them, adding a few bits of wood between the string and the future wale to act as a rough former for the additional curvature required round the bows. Leave the material tied up like this while you are making the frames or any other jobs, and by the time you are ready to use them you will find that the "wales" have taken on a "set" which will make working them round the hull a very simple matter. I much prefer this dry bending to using steamed timber, which must expand to some extent during steaming, only to contract again after it is in position.

However, assuming that the material for the wales is ready to go round the hull, and that one end has been fitted to go into the rabbet of the stem as already mentioned, this end should now be glued and dowelled in place and the clamps put on again. The end of the wale actually crosses the bottom of the knighthead, and when dowelling at this point run your dowels as near parallel to the stem as possible, in other words, "skew-dowel" the extreme end into the rabbet of the stem and the heel of the knighthead. This arrangement of skew-dowelling will be clear from *Sketch No. 45A* which shows the same principle applied to the ends of the planking. The line of the top of the wale was marked on the outer face of each frame as it was made, and these marks will now show the run of the wale throughout the length of the ship. Apply a spot of glue at the point on each of the first few frames where the wale will cross them, and, working from the bow, dowel the wale to each in turn, allowing the dowels to go right through and out the other side, holding the wale if necessary by means of simple clamps, although I did not use them, but worked the wale by hand as I went along. Continue glueing and dowelling to a few frames at a time until you reach the stern, where the wale should be cut off to the same bevel as the transom, but 1/8 in. short to allow for the transom-end-timber—*Sketches No. 35 and 47*—which will run up the side and cover the ends of the transom planking. When one wale is in position and the glue has had time to dry, fit the one on the other side, after which the top jig can be removed and the model taken from the jig and inspected at leisure, or for that matter viewed in the jig, which is after all the best, for one could hardly lift a ship off the building berth and take it up in the hands to look at it. The model will be worth looking at too, for here is no roughly shaped block of wood, still to be finished outside, but a complete ship ready for the outer skin of planking. At this stage you will begin to feel that it looks so good as it stands that it will be a shame to cover it with planking, and you will wonder whether it would not be a good idea to turn it into a model shipyard with a half finished ship on the stocks, rather than going on to complete the vessel herself. I know that I always pass through that phase at some stage of the construction, and perhaps someday I may try such a model, but then there are so many models I would like to build but will never have the time to do so. One thing is certain, when once you have experienced the pleasure of seeing a real ship grow under your hands like this, you will never again want to go back to the laminated or solid block method of modelling a wooden ship, it will seem too crude after the real thing.

We will now rest on our laurels for a while, feeling very satisfied with ourselves in general and the model in particular, and take this opportunity to look at a few tools. It occurs to me that, in making the list mentioned in Chapter I. I forgot one small but very useful tool, which I have in several shapes. I have suggested that it is always as well to allow all dowels to go right through the material to be joined and come out on the other side, in that way one is certain that they have gone fully home. This leaves a crop of dowel heads projecting into the hull at various points, and these have to be cut off. The most useful tool for this purpose is the very small jeweller's wire cutter, *Sketch No. 36*, and I would strongly advise the builder to get at least two pairs of these, one for end and the other for side cutting. As a matter of fact I have some with the cutting edges at angles, which are most helpful when cutting off dowels which have come through at difficult points in the hull, say low down in the after frames when the planking has gone on. In buying these tools it is essential to see that they have the cutting edge flush with the outer face of the jaws as in *No. 36A*, and not in the centre—*37B*. The former will trim the dowel flush with the wood, leaving no trace projecting, but the latter would of course leave a short stump.

I have several times referred to clamps for holding components in place during assembly, and it is always as well to have a few of these handy to take over when you want to have your hands free, or to hold something while the glue dries, but there is no need for these to be either elaborate or expensive, in fact I have generally found that the improvised clamp is in the main the most useful. I have a few simple clamps made up from some bits of 1/4 in. x 1/8 in. flat with a 3/16 in. screw through one side *Sketch No. 37*. I also made a few simple clamps from bits of hardwood bound with wire, which are also shown in the same sketch, but perhaps the most useful clips were those made as required from bits of spring wire, something on the same principle as the wire paper clip used for holding several sheets of correspondence together. Such clips can be bent to any shape and size, and there are very few jobs one cannot hold by means of a home-made wire clip. Of course there is no strength in any of the clips I have described, but then strength is not needed for such work as this. I have a great objection to any part of a "built" hull being forced into position and then held there against its will, such treatment not only puts a lot of unnecessary strain on the actual fixings, but also leaves the hull under constant stress. I like to feel that all the components of the model are at rest when they are in position, which is why in my own models I always insist on pre-bending, cold if possible, but steamed if not, so that the component, whether it be the wale, or a plank, will stay in position, or roughly so, without fixings. I like to feel that if I removed all the fixings from any part of the hull, the various pieces might fall apart, but they would retain their shape while doing so.

Your model is now framed, framed and built to scale, with only a very few and very minor departures from full-size practice, none of which will effect the external appearance of the job, which is more than can be said for the little model of the barquentine *Waterwitch* shown in *Fig*. 11. I have included this as an illustration of how a model should not appear, for it has several major faults, most of which I have already warned the reader to avoid. This little model was one of my first efforts to achieve that model with "real planks" in the hull, which had, been the boyish ambition mentioned in Chapter I., and I suppose that to a large extent I did manage what I set out to do, for there is much about this model which satisfies me even to this day. The lines are pleasing, more pleasing in reality than they appear in the reproduction, for the ends are very shapely. Care was taken to follow the different plank thicknesses between the topsides and the bulwarks, a feature of the wooden ship which is all too frequently overlooked in models. The deck is planked and the spars quite satisfactory, although spoiled by the furled sails being too heavy, but at that time I had not discovered the means to get over this difficulty. Unfortunately however, the internal work has rather neutralized these good points, for in this model I have used solid bulkheads which, as the plank fastenings indicate all too clearly, are placed at what to scale would be about five feet apart. Having placed these "frames" at such wide intervals, I should have used dowels made of the same material as the planking so that they would not have been conspicuous, or I should have painted over the hull. Instead I used metal fastenings and polished the hull. Today I would not dream of using "frames" so widely spaced, and on the subject of dowels versus metal fixings, at the time this model was built I had not discovered the former. The next fault is in the width of the planking, if those used in this job were reproduced full size, they would be over two feet wide midships, so the whole effect would have been improved had they been cut down to nearer scale size. Another point is that the fastenings in the forward ends of the hull planking are too far away from the stem, from which it is obvious that stem-doublers were used to take them. We will be using stem-doublers in the *Leon* model, but they will not be so heavy in relation to the scale of the vessel, and we will take care to keep the fastenings in the right place, not about a foot (scale size) out from the stem. In my opinion this little barquentine is a good example of an otherwise pleasing model, spoiled by a lack of attention to the effect internal construction can have on external appearance. It is one of the mistakes I am not now likely to repeat, but if its inclusion here can serve as a warning to future builders of such models, then we can at least say that it has earned its keep.

We can now return to the model in hand. After the main wales are in position the next job will be to fit the bilge-stringers, which add the final strength to the frames by tying them together along the line of the bilge an important feature if, as in the case of my own model, the planking is to be done with the model resting on the table and not held in a special jig. With the model out on the table it will be the turn of the bilge which will take all the knocks, and if the frames were only fixed at the keel and their upper ends, it is possible that some of them might be racked before the planking had gone far enough to protect them. When the bilge-stringers are in place however, the frames are locked along this projecting corner throughout their entire length.

In full-size practice these stringers would be incorporated in the ceiling when the latter ran all up the sides, or form the edge of it when it extended only over the bottom of the hold. In *Leon* the bilge-stringers are from 3/16 in. x 1/16 in, but any material about this size will do. Cut off a suitable length as shown on the plans and lay it inside the turn of the bilge on the midship frame where it is fixed with a spot of glue and dowelled. A small clamp is advisable to help the dowel until the stringer is held on a few more frames. Glue and dowel to the next frame forward, then the next aft, working outward from the centre all the time until it is fixed throughout its length. Do not attempt to force it into any particular curve, but let it take whatever shape it will providing it lies flat on the surface of the frames, as a matter of fact it will naturally follow quite closely the turn of the bilge. When fixing the bilge-stringer, do not worry about the dowels going right through they are soon cut off flush when all are in position. The stringer on the opposite side is put on in the same way, and when these two are in position you will be surprised at the strength of the whole framework.

The beam-shelf will be the next to go in, but before we fit it I feel that it might be as well to put in a word of warning to the model builder who is new to wooden ships. If you should be building some vessel other than *Leon*, do not follow the latter's arrangement regarding the fixing of the deck and beams without first checking that it does apply to the ship you are making. The use of the outside wale was not the most usual arrangement, the general practice being to fit the wale *inside* the frames and on top of the deck-beams, in which position it became the "waterway" as shown in *Sketches No.* 43, 73 *and* 74, which had the effect of placing the deck level much lower than it appeared to be when seen from the outside of the ship, whereas in *Leon* there was only the thickness of the covering-board between the actual deck level and the bottom of the bulwarks as viewed from outboard. However I will go more fully into this point a little later,

In *Leon* the top of the wale is flush with the top of the deck planking at the ship's side, so that the covering-board will sit comfortably on both, therefore the top of the beam-shelf will have to follow the top of the wale, and the thickness of the planking and beams below it. For fixing the shelf I used a simple jig as shown in *Sketch No.* 38, but, before actually dowelling in place, run the shelf in position, held here and there by a few clamps and mark the fore end where the flair of the bows causes it to "roll" slightly outwards, then dress down the upper surface so that it will be level

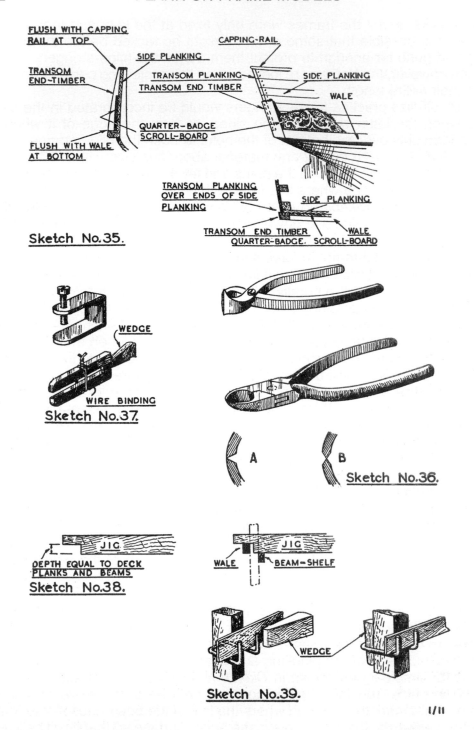

FLUSH WITH CAPPING RAIL AT TOP

SIDE PLANKING

TRANSOM END~TIMBER

CAPPING-RAIL

TRANSOM PLANKING
TRANSOM END TIMBER

SIDE PLANKING

WALE

QUARTER—BADGE
SCROLL—BOARD

FLUSH WITH WALE AT BOTTOM

TRANSOM PLANKING OVER ENDS OF SIDE PLANKING

SIDE PLANKING

Sketch No. 35.

TRANSOM END TIMBER
QUARTER-BADGE. SCROLL-BOARD

WALE

WEDGE

WIRE BINDING

Sketch No. 37.

A   B

Sketch No. 36.

JIG

DEPTH EQUAL TO DECK PLANKS AND BEAMS

Sketch No. 38.

WALE

JIG

BEAM—SHELF

WEDGE

Sketch No. 39.

to receive the underside of the beams, after which it can be glued and dowelled in position, using the jig already mentioned for the purpose of keeping it in true relation with the wale. Incidentally I found a few simple "clamps" as *Sketch No.* 39, extremely useful for holding wale, shelves, and planking to the frames, they were made from bits of hard steel wire and wooden wedges. When the shelves are in, the forward ends should be joined by means of a breast-hook, although in a model which is to be fully planked its fitting is a matter of taste. If your pleasure lies in building the model rather than seeing the finished product, then you will fit it, even though no one will see it when the job is finished; if on the other hand you get no particular pleasure out of fitting it, then there is no reason why it should not be omitted. It is all a matter of the particular angle from which you approach modelling. It is not a question of having any desire to know that a model is true to the original even in those parts which cannot be seen, but merely that for me the pleasure is in making things rather than in possessing them when once they are made, and any internal work I put in a model is really for the pleasure of doing it, not for the knowledge that it is there.

I have already mentioned that it was common practice to flll in the spaces between the first few cant-frames on either side of the bow, and I fitted solid blocks between the frames on the stem and stern-post. These filling chocks, or doublers, were fitted to the stem as in *Sketch No.* 34, and to the stern-post as shown in the wash-drawings, *Fig.* 6 *and* 13. These latter drawings by the way are not of the *Leon* model but of a vessel having a much shorter counter, hawse-holes in the bulwarks and several other differences, but they serve to illustrate a number of constructional details used in the *Leon.* The filling-chocks are of course both glued and dowelled in position.

With the beam-shelves glued and dowelled to each frame, and the filling-chocks on either side of the stem and stern-posts, we have now to decide whether to fit the deck beams at this stage or after planking. If they are put in they strengthen the whole frame, but on the other hand if you intend to plank the model, as I like to do, just in the hands or resting on the table, then the fact of being able to get your hand inside the hull instead of an odd finger thrust between closely spaced beams, is a great advantage, and I am rather in favour of planking before putting in the beams, There is also the advantage of being able to get at the heads of any dowels which may project into the hull. With the beams in place it can be very difficult to get at such dowels to cut them off.

The question of whether in certain jobs one should use short dowels which do not project on the other side, or drill the hole right through and let all dowels project, to be cut off later, is one which I have never settled to my complete satisfaction. Of course in such jobs as jointing frames, keel, keelson, etc., there is no doubt whatever, the dowels should go right through wherever possible, but in small jobs like fixing planking, there seems to me to be much to be said for both methods. Short dowels with the holes drilled only to the required depth are on the whole the best, but in using them one must mark the dowelling before inserting it and cutting off, otherwise there is a risk that it may not be driven far enough to drive out the pocket of compressed air which must be formed as the dowel goes in. Dowels going right through are easier to drive since the bottom of the hole is open, also one does not need to bother about length, for one drives until the end appears on the other side of the wood. The short dowels leave the frames looking neater on the inside, but there really is not much in this, for with the dowels cut off flush they will not show to any great extent, in fact no more than they do on the outside of the planking. On the question of strength I do not think there is anything to choose between them. I certainly do not think the long dowel in any way weakens the frame, providing that the same drill has been used for both making the dowel and drilling the hole, and that the dowel has been dipped in knotting before being driven. Such dowels become part of the original fabric. I proved that with a model which had been damaged during the war and which I broke up just to see what its condition was really like. I found that a frame would break between dowels rather than along the line of the dowel itself, the bamboo, stuck with knotting to the wood about it, was in fact stronger than the material used to make the frame. Of course it would have been a different story if the dowel had been the wrong size for the hole, or had been driven without knotting. It is possible that under such circumstances the frame would have split along the hole. However one does not as a rule build models for the purpose of testing them to destruction, and I am convinced that under all normal conditions the life of a dowelled job will be much longer than that of one having metal fixings. Dowels become part of the material into which they are driven, whereas metal will always remain a foreign body, and should the wood get very dry, the latter will become slack, I have two good examples of that among the models in my own little collection.

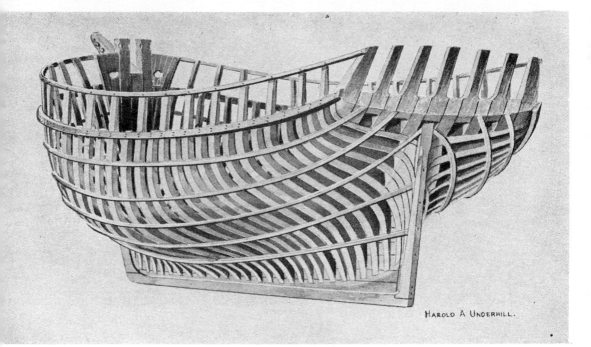

Fig. 6.
PLANKING-BATTENS IN POSITION.

Fig. 7.
Deck Beams Fitted.

1/8 in. SCALE MODEL OF *LEON* BY PROFESSOR FAVEZ.

Fig. 8.
Planking-Battens Fitted.

CHAPTER III

PLANKING THE HULL

THE run of the external planking is perhaps the most important feature of a plank-built model, it can make or mar the whole effect. Further it is possible to produce a model in which the sweep of the planks appear perfect when seen from full broadside, but which results in some nasty curves when viewed from either bow or stern. Another very common fault which is liable to develop, is to find when the hull is half planked that there will be room for say nine or ten planks midships, but only six or seven forward or aft. This can well happen even if the run of planking has all been worked out before hand, since it only requires the slightest fraction too much width left on the ends of say five or six planks, to throw the whole thing out in the final stages. This is one reason why I do not like the run of the planking worked out on paper, but of that more later. Of course with some hull forms it is quite impossible to run the planking evenly fore and aft, or for that matter to get in the same number of planks at the ends as you have midships, unless the ends are to be made so narrow that there will not be room for the fastenings, but under such circumstances special "stealers" are worked in to overcome the difficulty. This however is a very different matter to finding, when the hull is half planked, that the requisite number of strakes cannot be got on the stem. If stealers are to be used they should be worked in where they will maintain the natural sweep of the planking, and not as a means of correcting an error discovered when it is too late to do anything else, in fact if the planking has got well up the topsides before the need for them is discovered, it would be better to strip the hull down to the level of the bilge and start again, working in stealers low down, about on the line of the planks which have to run off the curve of thc bilge and flatten out into the stem or stern-posts. Above the waterline the run of the strakes should more or less follow the sweep of the sheer. However if you lay your planking with care, and by the means which I will describe, there will be no risk of the strakes running off or of stealers being required, other than where legitimately necessary to cope with certain hull forms, and in these cases they will automatically fall in the correct places.

One can work out the run of the planking by means of an "expanded"

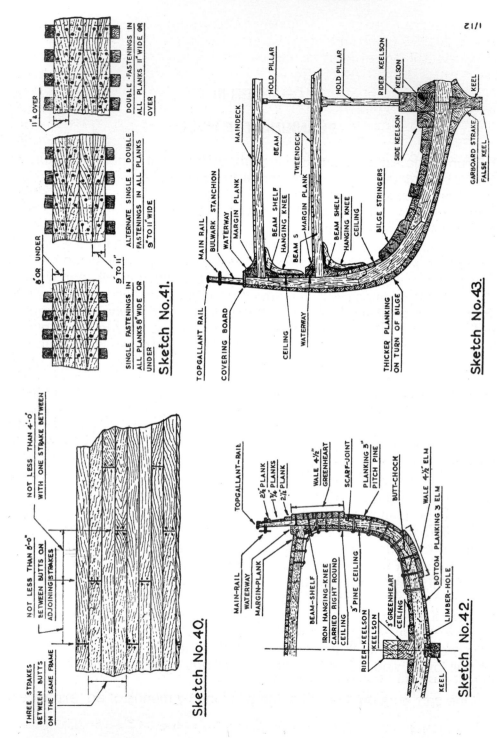

1/12

Sketch No.41.

DOUBLE ·FASTENINGS IN ALL PLANKS 11" WIDE OR OVER

11" & OVER

ALTERNATE SINGLE & DOUBLE FASTENINGS IN ALL PLANKS 9" TO 11" WIDE

9" TO 11"

SINGLE FASTENINGS IN ALL PLANKS 8" WIDE OR UNDER

8" OR UNDER

Sketch No.43.

HOLD PILLAR
HOLD PILLAR
RIDER KEELSON
KEELSON
KEEL
MAINDECK
BEAM
TWEENDECK
SIDE KEELSON
GARBOARD STRAKE
FALSE KEEL
BULWARK STANCHION
MARGIN PLANK
BEAM SHELF
HANGING KNEE
BEAM S
MARGIN PLANK
BEAM SHELF
HANGING KNEE
CEILING
BILGE STRINGERS
MAIN RAIL
WATERWAY
TOPGALLANT RAIL
COVERING BOARD
CEILING
WATERWAY
THICKER PLANKING ON TURN OF BILGE

Sketch No.40.

NOT LESS THAN 4'-0" WITH ONE STRAKE BETWEEN

NOT LESS THAN 5'-0" BETWEEN BUTTS ON ADJOINING STRAKES

THREE STRAKES BETWEEN BUTTS ON THE SAME FRAME

Sketch No.42.

TOPGALLANT-RAIL
2¾" PLANK
1¾" PLANKS
2½" PLANK
WALE 4½" GREENHEART
SCARF-JOINT
PLANKING 5" PITCH PINE
BUTT-CHOCK
WALE 4½" ELM
MAIN-RAIL
WATERWAY
MARGIN-PLANK
BEAM-SHELF
IRON HANGING-KNEE CARRIED RIGHT ROUND CEILING
3" PINE CEILING
3" GREENHEART CEILING
RIDER-KEELSON
KEELSON
BOTTOM PLANKING 3 ELM
LIMBER-HOLE
KEEL

planking diagram, just as the modern shipyard will work out an expanded shell plating diagram, and this is a most interesting little job on the drawing board, but not one which the average model builder, with no ship design experience, is likely to wish to undertake. In any case as I have already said, planking from such a drawing still does not avoid the possibility of the planks running out of truth due to infinitesimal error in width on each of a large number of them. Your old shipwright would have scorned the idea of using a planking diagram, and would have run everything without drawings of any kind. Of course in his case he had years of experience behind him, but even so he had rough guides on the hull which enabled him to plank it section by section, and this is the method I apply to my own models, one which, if properly handled, makes faulty planking impossible.

However before going on with the planking of the model perhaps we should have a look at the regulations which governed the run of the strakes in a full-size merchant ship, for after all that is what we are out to represent, and therefore those simple rules are well worth keeping in mind. The various Ship Classification Societies have hard and fast rules under which ships must be built if they are to be accepted by them for registration, and as neither shippers nor insurance companies are likely to regard with enthusiasm any vessel refused classification, this is important. The rules are very extensive and cover the thickness and type of wood to be used for every component, and the estimated life of the various different timbers used in different places, but the only rule governing planking which is likely to be of interest to the model builder, is that which lays down the minimum distances allowed between the joints, or butts as they are termed, on adjacent frames or strakes, and the number of fastenings to be used in planks of various widths. The following is an extract from the rules under which ships were built in the 70's, when wood construction was perhaps at its height.

"No butts to be nearer than 5 ft. of each other unless there be a strake wrought between them, in which case a distance of 4 ft. will be allowed.

No butts to be on the same timber (frame) unless there be three strakes between them".

This rule has been shown diagrammatically in *Sketch No. 40* which should make it clear.

On the subject of fastenings the rule was that single fastenings, either bolts or tree-nails, could be used in planks 8 in. wide or under. For planks over 8 in. but not more than 11 in. wide the fastenings had to be not less than single and double on alternate timbers, while for all planks over 11 in. wide, double fastenings had to be used throughout. This rule is illustrated in *Sketch No. 41*.

This latter rule is one on which I think the model maker will have to use his own discretion, much will depend upon the scale of the model, and for small scale work I think it better to use a single dowel of reasonable proportions rather than trying to work in two extremely fine ones. Not that there is any lack of strength in bamboo dowels, but the surface area in contact with the inside face of the hole in the plank is very small.

However to return to *Leon*. In this ship the planking was flush externally from the covering-board down, but this does not mean that it was all of the same thickness, but merely that it had been increased and decreased in thickness gradually, the whole then having been planed smooth. The planking along the bilge and about the garboards would certainly be thicker than that used immediately above the bilge, but as the Lines Drawing for this model has been drawn to the outside of the planking, this will not affect us, and planking of one thickness will be used throughout.

This difference between the thickness of planking in different parts of the hull is rarely shown in models, yet it is a most important matter, and should be shown where it is known to exist in the original ship. *Sketch No.* 42 is from the midship section on the builders' drawings of the schooner *Mary Ashburner*, from which it will be seen that while the main planking was 3 in. thick, several strakes on the turn of the bilge were increased to 4½ in. thick, as were the last few strakes in the topsides. It will also be noticed that in *Sketch No.* 43 the ceiling is increased in thickness along the turn of the bilge where these thicker strakes served the purpose of the bilge-stringer in *Leon*. The thickening of the planking on the bilge and topsides served a dual purpose, for it not only acted like the webs of a girder and stiffened the hull top and bottom, but it also gave additional thickness at levels which were likely to come in contact with other objects, the bilge with the ground when the ship was high and dry, and the topsides with other vessels, or a quay wall, in fact these thicker planks acted as rubbing strakes, which explains why this type of planking was so commonly used in smaller craft such as coasting schooners, vessels which were more frequently in port than the larger deep-water craft.

As far as I could see in *Leon*, the bilge and garboard planking was increased in thickness, although planed down to blend into the topsides, while the external wale served as a rubbing strake in place of thicker planking at that level. *Sketch No.* 43 is the midship section of a larger vessel, in which the differences have been planed off. This incidentally shows that a builders' Lines Drawing of a wooden ship does not necessarily show the true shape of the hull, since the varying thicknesses of planking can in fact produce an entirely different shape to that on the frames. This is particularly noticeable at the keel in *Sketch No.* 43. However the possibility of the modeller having an original Lines Plan of a wooden merchant ship is fairly remote, since most of these vessels, at least in the smaller classes, were built from half models, not from plans. When Lines Drawings were used a constructional midship section as *Sketch No.* 42 was generally added to indicate the differences between the frames and the planking.

From this it will be seen that for the model builder a plan drawn to the outside of the planking has its advantages, since it allows him to use planking of whatever thickness suits him and to make his frames accordingly. However to return to the model. The first point is to settle the run of the planks, and for this cut a number of thin battens—I had strips fo some 1/16 in. square sycamore which proved ideal for the *Leon* model each long enough to go round the hull at the turn of the bilge. Now take one of these strips and pin the centre of it on the midship frame right on the turn of the bulge, sweep it round the hull so that it rests nicely of the turn of the bilge all the way, fixing it to every second or third frame on the way—at this stage some of your home-made wire clips may hold it. Do not force it, but let it follow its own natural sweep so that one face makes contact with each frame. Having settled this curve, lightly tack it to every second frame and to the stem and stern-posts. Now take up another strip and run it in the same way between the first batten and the keel, and then run another between the first and the wale. Further battens can be added between those already fixed, the number used depending upon the size of the model you are building, but the more you put on the more accurate will be the planking when you come to run it. I usually finish with about 3/4 in. or 1 in. between battens for models up to say 1/8 in. scale, and not more than 2 in. for larger craft.

When all battens are in position take the model up in your hands and examine it from all angles—with a large model you will of course have to leave it on its jig and walk round it—to see that the sweep of the battens is fair from all points of view. It is probable that they will not be at the first trial, for you are almost certain to have arranged your battens at equal spacing all along the hull, and this does not necessarily give the best running strakes, since to achieve this it is often desirable that the planks taper more quickly in some parts of the hull than others in the same vertical plane. So if from some angles the curves are not all you would wish, adjust the ends of the battens and try again, taking care of course, that you do not put too much taper in any one section. When at last quite satisfied that you have no bad curves in your battens, and that you have got the best possible arrangement, fix a similar set to the opposite side, measuring their positions from those already fixed, and at this stage your model should look like that in the wash-drawing *Fig.* 6 and the photographs *Figs.* 8, 9 *and* 10. In this particular model the battens have been tied or wired in position, but I usually use fine naturalist pins—or "bug-pins" as they are more vulgarly called—made for the purpose of mounting butterflies, insects, etc., and obtainable in very small sizes.

We have now arrived at what I always think a very fascinating stage of building, that of planking the hull, but before getting down to work, see that you have made a good supply of dowelling of the requisite size. The question of where you start planking, either at the wale or the keel is a matter of taste, so I think we will start at the wale, although in the model shown in the wash-drawing *Fig.* 13 the garboard strake was the first put on. The first thing to settle is the width of planking to be used, and I would suggest that a scale of 12 in. for the maximum width of average planks would be about right, although there may be an odd strake, say down near the stern-post where this may be exceeded, as it might in full-size practice. I managed to buy some strips of 3/16 in. x 1/16 in. which was used for most of the work, with a few lengths of 1/4 in. x 1/16 in. for cutting planks with a fair amount of curvature, and as the scale of the *Leon* model is 1/8 in. this proved ample.

In a small model the planks which run out to the transom could if desired be put on in one piece, but no shipyard would have planks about 120 ft. long, nor could they handle them if they had, so if you are building a scale model your planks must be restricted to lengths within scale limits, say up to about 3 in. on a 1/8 in. scale model. Of course the same thing could be said of the wale, bilge-stringer and beam-shelf, for strictly speaking these too should be put on in scale lengths, but these are items in which I think the additional strength of one continuous piece of timber outweighs the value of scale accuracy, although in a large model one would score the face of the wale to represent the joints and put in dummy dowels on either side of them. This is a simple matter, and strength is essential if, as in the case of my own models, the hull is going to be planked either held in the hand or lying on a bench. I prefer to have the model quite free while planking, not held in a jig, so that it can be turned this way and that to give the best approach for drilling holes and driving dowels, and so that one can get one's hands either inside or outside the model with equal ease. This often saves the use of clamps which tend to get in the way when finally dowelling the strakes, although they can be very useful to hold a plank while fitting its edge, and for this purpose I find the simple wire clamp shown in *Sketch No.* 39 very satisfactory. It can be used in two ways, either with the wedge on the face of the plank when one is likely to want to move it about during early fitting, or with the wedge inside the frame when drilling holes and dowelling. However as I have already said, I dispense with the use of clamps to a large extent, although they are useful things to have around the place in case you want your hands free for some odd job, or have to leave a plank before it is properly fixed.

I have already advised the reader to invest in a pair of proportional dividers *Sketch No.* 7, and if he has done so he will find them a great saving in time when planking, as well as an added aid to accuracy, but for the moment we will assume that he does not have this most useful instrument. The first stage is to divide the midship frame between the wale and the centre of the first batten into the number of planks which have to go into this space. For example, supposing the space to be 1⅛ in., then it would divide into nine 1/8 in. planks, but if it is say 1¹⁄₁₆ in., then it will be divided into nine planks of just under 1/8 in. wide. Do the same on either side of midships, marking out nine—or as many as your model requires—equal spaces between the wale and the centre of the batten on the face of every second frame, so that you now have the plank widths on every second frame for the whole belt contained between the wale and the first batten. For the remaining belts the space to be divided will of course be from centre to centre of battens, except for the last one, which will be measured from the centre of the batten to the bottom of the rabbet of the keel. The stem and stern-post will of course also be divided out between the ends of the battens in the same way. If you have a pair of proportional dividers then none of this dividing and marking of the frames will be necessary, since it will be possible to set these divisions directly on each plank as it is about to be cut, as will be described later.

Before actually cutting any planks it is as well to see just where you want your joints, or butts, to come to agree with the rules quoted at the beginning of this chapter. It is no use just running 3 in. lengths until you come to the end of the row, and then finding that you are left with a plank which will only cover two timbers. A lot of trouble can be saved by making a very rough diagram of each belt of planking. Such a diagram need not be to scale or even drawn with a rule or straight-edge, all you need is a series of vertical lines representing the number of frames in the model, then across these draw lines representing the number of planks in the first belt—nine in the hypothetical example already quoted—and on this work out where the joints should come, putting a cross on each vertical line to indicate the joints. When the first line is marked out do the second and so on. Your first arrangement may not work out quite right, well it is easy to rub out the crosses and try the joints on another set of frames. When the first belt has been worked out continue with the next, remembering of course that the continuity of arrangement must be carried right through, for in the finished model there will be no separate belts of planking, so the hull must be treated as a whole. In making this diagram you simply decide how many frames an average plank would cover, which in the case of the *Leon* model would be about eight or nine, then divide this into the total number of frames in the ship, which gives you the number of planks in the first strake. If the result should be say four and one-eighth planks, then you would obviously either increase the lengths of each to make it four, or reduce two of them so that you had three of normal length and two of medium length. You would not reduce every plank so that you had five of equal length, since in full-size practice that would merely represent a waste of timber. Move down to the next strake and place the joints so that they are at least five feet apart—say three frames in *Leon*—but more if possible while still keeping the planks of suitable lengths, and so on down your diagram. Keep this sketch by you, and as you fix each strake, mark the frames which have to have a butt, and you cannot go wrong. This may sound rather complicated, but it is not really, and a little trial and error on your slip of paper will soon put things right.

When once you have settled the location of the butts you are ready to start planking. Let us assume that your first butt will fall on frame six, then cut a piece of timber rather longer than required and hold it against the frames so that it makes good contact all along, at the same time pressing it against the underside of the wale with the forward end in the rabbet of the stem. Mark the angle of the rabbet on the end of the plank and cut it to this. Put the forward end back into the rabbet and again offer the top of the plank to the wale—a bulldog clip is often useful for holding the end of the plank in the rabbet at this stage—and if it does not make good contact all the way, run a pencil along the underside of the wale to mark the top edge of the plank, which is then removed and trimmed to this line. This by the way is one of the advantages in using short planks, for the curvature in any single length is so slight that very little fitting is required. Try the plank in place again and if, as it should, it will now lie in good contact with all the frames, sit properly in the rabbet of the stem, and rest cleanly against the underside of the wale it is ready for final cutting. Fix it in position, either with clamps or by holding it with the fingers, and pencil across it the centres of the frames it crosses, the last pencil line representing the butt or joint with the next plank, to which it should then be cut. Take care with this cut, for the finished end must he exactly on the centre of the frame, since your next plank must also make a landing on this with sufficient room for the fixing. Alternatively a Scarf Joint in the thickness of the plank may be used. On the face of your frames you have marked the width of the planks which cross them, and also the widths at the stem, so take a small piece of stiff paper and a very sharp pencil, and on the edge of the paper mark the plank width at the stem, transfer this width to the fore-end of the plank. Do the same for the width at the first frame, and transfer this to the first pencil line across your plank, and so on until the width at each frame crossing is marked on the plank, measuring of course from the top edge of the plank in each case. When all these marks are on, run a pencil line through them and you have the shape of the lower edge of the plank, which should then be cut to it. Try the plank in place, and if it has been properly cut. the lower edge should just rest on the pencil marks

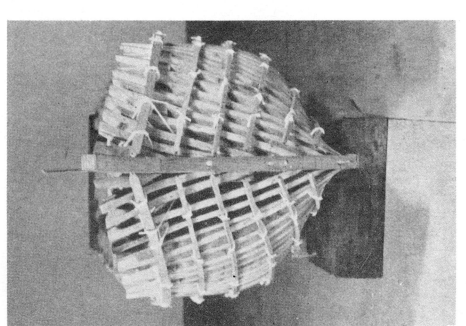

Fig. 9.
Bow View.

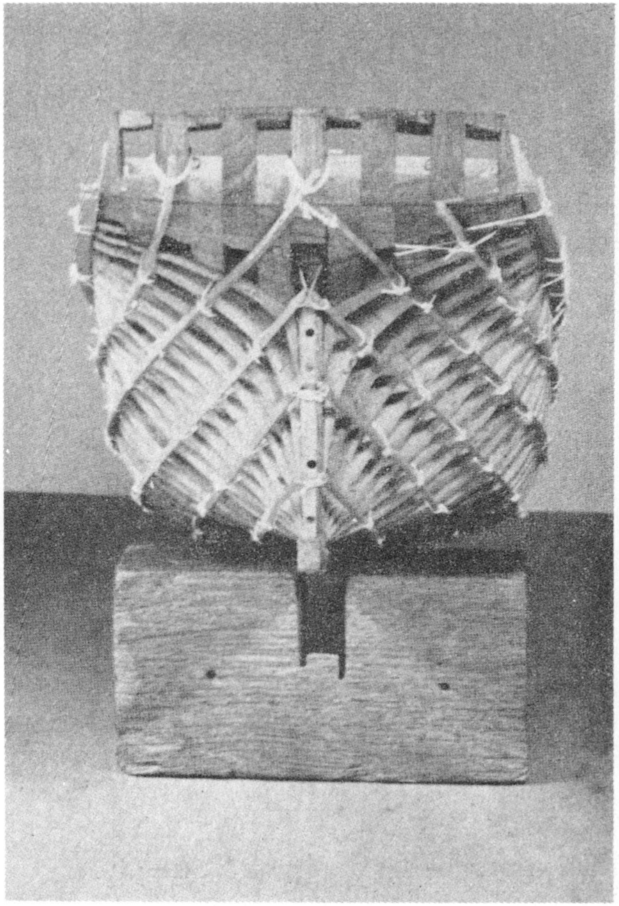

Fig. 10.
Stern, showing Stern frame.

PLANKING-BATTENS ON PROFESSOR FAVEZ'S MODEL OF *LEON*

Fig, 11.
A SMALL SCALE
MODEL
BY THE AUTHOR.

An early effort, showing how a model should *not* be built.

Fig.12.

Another early model by the author with whom the barquentine rig has been popular.

on the frame when the top edge is in position against the wale and the forward end in the rabbet of the stem. If everything is correct, use this plank as a template, and with a very sharp pencil mark out another like it for use on the opposite side of the hull. I think the most important item in setting out planks in this way is that you should be able to sharpen a pencil properly, and it is surprising how many people seem unable to do this! Planks set out with a blunt point will "creep" to such an extent that they will be completely out by the time the first half-dozen strakes are in position. If you cannot make a needle-sharp point on a pencil, then use the point of a needle inserted in a pen holder.

Now let us see the same job done with proportional dividers. The fitting of the plank to the underside of the wale and into the rabbet of the stem is of course the same, and the lines representing the centres of the frames crossed by this plank are drawn on its face as before, but there will have been no need to have marked the faces of the frames with the number of planks required, or to lift these dimensions off the frames and transfer them to the plank, all that preliminary work can be omitted. Let us assume that it has been decided to fit eight planks between the underside of the wale and the centre of the first batten, then you set the centre screw on your dividers to "8", which means that there is a ratio of 8 to 1 between the two ends of the instrument, so having fitted the upper edge of your plank to the wale, you simply place one point of the long end of the dividers against the underside of the wale in the rabbet of the stem, and the other where the centreline of the first batten enters the rabbet, turn the instrument over and lay one point on the upper edge of the plank, and the other point will indicate the depth of the plank at that point. Mark this then move to the first frame, open the wide end to the space to be covered on this frame, and with the short end mark the width of the plank on the pencil line representing the crossing of that frame. Repeat this on each frame in turn and you will have a series of dots which represent the true shape of the lower edge. *Sketch No. 44* will make all this quite clear.

There is another advantage in using these dividers for setting out the planking, and that is, should any slight error be made in the actual cutting of the planks after marking out, the dividers will automatically correct this in succeeding strakes, since when once the first strake has been laid fore and aft, the dividers will be reset to the number of strakes remaining to be fitted in that particular belt. In the example used here, that means that when fitting the second strake down from the wale the dividers would be set at "7", for the third strake "6" and so on. In other words, each space is treated independently and on its own merits.

You now have your first plank ready to fit, but before doing so bend it in your fingers to something like the curvature of the hull at the place where it is to be fitted, and you will find it will retain that curve, resting on

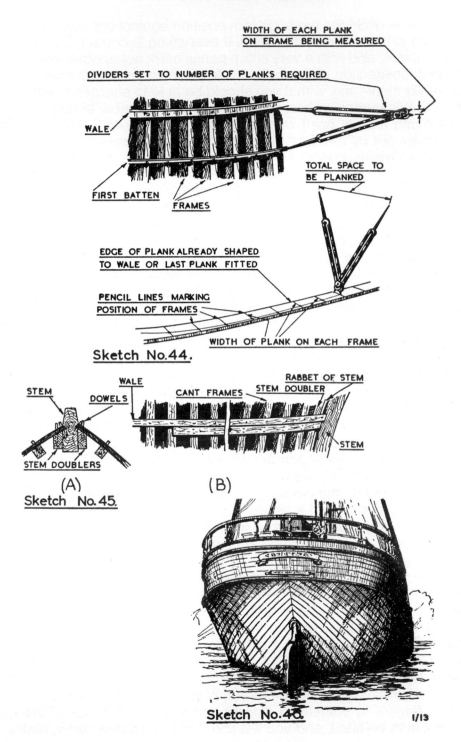

WIDTH OF EACH PLANK
ON FRAME BEING MEASURED

DIVIDERS SET TO NUMBER OF PLANKS REQUIRED

WALE

FIRST BATTEN

FRAMES

TOTAL SPACE TO
BE PLANKED

EDGE OF PLANK ALREADY SHAPED
TO WALE OR LAST PLANK FITTED

PENCIL LINES MARKING
POSITION OF FRAMES

WIDTH OF PLANK ON EACH FRAME

Sketch No. 44.

STEM

DOWELS

STEM DOUBLERS

(A)

WALE

CANT FRAMES

RABBET OF STEM

STEM DOUBLER

STEM

(B)

Sketch No. 45.

Sketch No. 46.

1/13

the frames without any tendency to spring away at either end, after a little practice you will be able to set the various planks to just the curves you require. With a fine brush—a child's paint brush is just the thing—put a little glue in the rabbet of the stem; on the face of each frame to be covered; also along the underside of the wale and the top edge of the plank, then feed the plank into position, where a bulldog clip at the stem and a couple of the wire clips on the frames will hold it while you take up your drill. I usually use a small pin-chuck *Sketch No.* 31 for drilling the holes for planking, so having selected the right drill for the dowel being used, remove the bulldog clip, and holding the end of the plank into the rabbet with your thumb, drill the hole for the dowel going into the rabbet, dip the end of a length of dowelling into some knotting, push into the hole, break off and then drive home, leaving a little projecting to be cut off later. Watch that the plank is still in good contact with the wale, and proceed to drill and dowel to the filling chuck on the side of the stem—this might also be called the "stem-doubler" or "apron". This last dowel should be driven parallel to the stem and not square with the plank, as shown in *Sketch No.* 45A. This locks the hood-end of the plank more securely than would a square dowel. Proceed to dowel the plank to all frames, working from forward, then cut off all dowel heads, after which your first plank should appear as in *Sketch* No. 45B although the question of whether you have used one or two dowels per frame will depend upon the size of model or width of plank. Next fit the same plank on the opposite side of the ship, the plank which you marked out from the one just fitted. When these two are on, fit the next pair aft in the same way, and do not under any circumstances be tempted to run a whole length of planking on one side, but always fit a plank on one side, then its opposite number on the other. In this way not only will you ensure that both sides of the ship are alike, but also avoid any risk of the ship being pulled out of shape by planking one side only. I know only too well the desire to see several planks on just to get the general effect, but do not give way to it, for it may only lead to a rather unsatisfactory job in the end.

When you get aft near the counter, the planks tend to twist under the stern, so that you will have to sharply bevel the top edge to make it fit closely under the wale, while the lower edge will require to be bevelled to meet the plank below it, but all this will work out quite automatically by feeding the edge of the plank to the wale and trimming it until it will rest properly against it, while the lower edge will be bevelled until it stands out square from the frame. Incidentally, after each plank has been dowelled, take a razor blade and carefully scrape away any glue which may be showing outside it, for if left to get dry this can be a lot of trouble, particularly in the rabbet of the stem, when you come to lay the adjoining plank. The edge of each plank should be glued to the one already fixed.

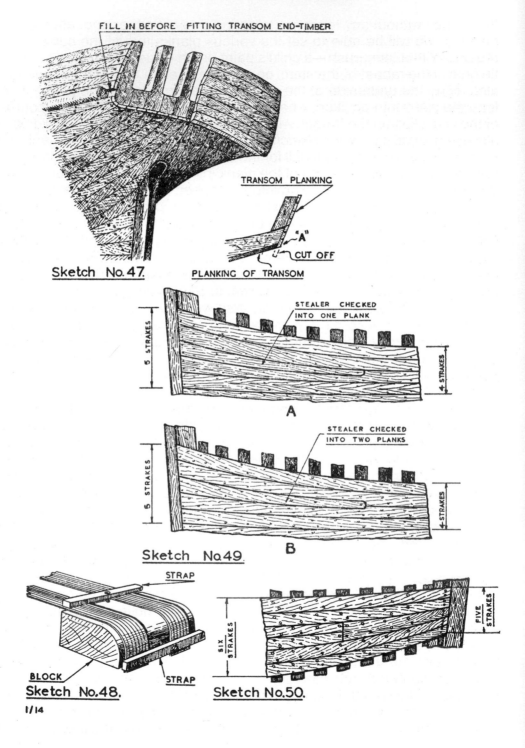

FILL IN BEFORE FITTING TRANSOM END-TIMBER

Sketch No. 47.

TRANSOM PLANKING

"A"

CUT OFF

PLANKING OF TRANSOM

STEALER CHECKED INTO ONE PLANK

5 STRAKES

4 STRAKES

A

STEALER CHECKED INTO TWO PLANKS

5 STRAKES

4 STRAKES

Sketch No. 49.

B

STRAP

STRAP

BLOCK

Sketch No. 48.

1/14

SIX STRAKES

FIVE STRAKES

Sketch No. 50.

The first one or two strakes below the wale run out over the transom aft, and for that reason may be worked from bow to stern as just described, but as soon as the planks below the counter begin to meet those from the opposite side of the ship, or to end in the rabbet of the stern-post, then the practice of starting with the first plank at the bow and finishing with the last one at the stern will come to an end, and in each strake we will first fix the plank adjoining the stem, then that which has either to meet below the counter or be fitted into the rabbet of the stern-post, finally filling in between these two. There is a very good reason for this. So long as the planking runs out to the edge of the transom, then the last one to be fitted can be left a little long, and cut off flush with the face of the transom later, but as soon as both ends of the strake have to end in *fitted* shape, this cannot be done, and it is advisable to get these "fitted" ends in first, so that the last plank to go into the strake is midships, where it will have simple square ends which can easily be trimmed or filed down until the plank will just push into place between those on either side. If you doubt the advantage of this, I can only suggest that you try running a full strake in which the closing plank—the last to go on—is that which has to be fitted into the rabbet of the stern-post, which, thanks to the upward swing of the strakes in the run, it will meet at a sharp angle. Try fitting this angle with the forward end of the plank locked against the butt of the last plank fitted, and you will be left in no doubt as to the benefit of making the rabbeted ends first.

Underneath the counter the planks meet in a mitred joint, *Sketches No. 46 and* 47, which is another reason for fitting the planks on alternate sides of the ship, since nothing looks worse than to see the planks at this point meeting in unequal angles, or even with their seams slightly staggered. These mitred ends meet on the solid portion of the stern-frame immediately abaft the rudder trunk, *Sketch No.* 24. Different ships have different sterns, and the run of the planking at this stage will largely depend upon the shape of the counter. The transom-counter with its wide almost flat end, such as that of *Leon*, is perhaps the most difficult to plank, owing to the very sharp roll immediately below the wale, but when once the first one or two strakes below this are in position, the rest of the hull will offer no difficulty, and I found this model extremely simple to plank, with, in my case, no need for stealers in any part of the hull. I say "in my case" because it does not always follow that the same hull will be planked quite the same by different people, in fact if I were to build another one myself from the same plans, I might not arrive at quite the same run of plank, although as I know the curves I like, it is probable that it would be very nearly the same. Everything depends on the builder's layout of the battens in the first place, and very little difference in the placing of the ends of these would decide whether stealers will be required or not. There is no objection to stealers, in the right places, the main thing is to get good easy sweeps for the run of strakes, sweeps which will as far as possible, allow the planks to follow the curves of the hull naturally and without too much shaping or twisting, and if to obtain this end stealers are necesssry, then stealers are good practice. They are only bad when it is obvious that they have been put in to correct badly run planking, however as there should be no need for them in the topsides, we will leave their fitting until later.

Having run the top strake below the wale, and followed on with those immediately below it on either side of the hull, you arrive at the point where there is only room for one strake between the last one fitted and the centre of the first batten, so the latter should be stripped off, and using the pin holes it will have left in the frames as a guide for widths, cut out and fix the planks of this strake, which completes the first belt of planking on both sides of the ship. The next belt will be measured from the edge of the last strake fitted to the centre of the next batten, but we will not actually run this belt for some time yet. The next belt of planking to be fitted will be that from the keel up to the first batten above it. This again is a matter of expediency, and there is no hard and fast rule why it should be done this way, but if once you try planking straight through from keel to rail, or from rail to keel, and then try planking from both top and bottom and meeting in the middle, I do not think you will have any doubts about the advantages of the latter. The plank with the least curvature in the whole hull is that mid-ships on the turn of the bilge, it is in fact almost invariably dead straight and without any taper, so what better one could be imagined as the clos-ing piece in the jig-saw of the external planking? What is more it is the most easy to get at for both fitting and dowelling. I said when we started that there is no reason why the builder should not have started with the garboard strake, that next to the keel, and worked up, finishing this belt before moving to the belt forming the topsides, but I am convinced that the method suggested is the best, particularly for a beginner. Except perhaps for the last plank in each of the top two strakes in this particular model, the topside planking is undoubtedly more simple to run than the lower belt, and it is therefore better that the builder get his hand in on this part of the work, so I still say "start below the wale".

We will assume that the builder has now planked the topside belt down to and including the first batten, so we will move down to the gar-board strake. From the rough diagram we made before we started plank-ing, we know just where the butts will have to be placed in this belt, so we can mark the frames to show where they fall in this first strake. We also know just how many strakes we have to lay in this belt, so we either divide out the frames accordingly, or set our dividers to the number required. Cut off a piece of planking material a little longer than required to reach the frame on which the butt is to land and proceed to offer it up to the rabbet in both stem and keel, after having given it the necessary "set" by bending it in your fingers. When it fits the rabbet properly, pencil on the frame centres, then set out the widths at these points as in the case of the other planks fitted, after which it can be glued and dowelled in position. These planks of the garboard strake will have considerable curvature and twist, and I think it most important that this should be put in each plank before fixing, for I like to feel that as built, my models are free from all internal stress, that each component is completely at rest and not depending upon the fastenings to retain its shape. In my models the fastenings are there to keep the various pieces from falling apart, but not to prevent them going out of shape. This "set" can be put into the planks cold, at least in a small model, but if there is much spring in the material used, it is sometimes an advantage to give it a pre-bending in some form of rough jig such as that shown in *Sketch No.* 48, the size and shape of which will depend upon the general average of the bends likely to be required, although there is no objection to a little over bending.

When the first plank of the garboard strake is in position at the bow on either side, move aft and fit that adjacent to the stern-post in the same way, afterwards filling in the planks between until the strake is complete, still working one plank on either side of the ship of course. Carry on in this way up to the level of the first batten, which is then removed. Incidentally, the garboard strake is not only dowelled to the frames, but also to the rabbet of the keel between the frames, also the ends of these planks will be glued for the full extent of their contact with the deadwood at either end, which brings to mind another point. Many of the frames in the after end of the ship will not extend as far as the keel down the sides of the deadwood, so their centrelines should be pencilled on the latter and the planks dowelled on these lines. This will ensure that the dowels run in straight vertical lines right down the side of the ship from rail to keel, while if these lines are not put in, the dowels in the planks on the deadwood will probably wander all over the place and look very untidy in the finished model.

When this lower belt of planking is in, one may either continue with the belt immediately above it, or move to the second belt on the topsides, but whichever you decide, always do one above and one below, so that the last strake of all to go in the ship will be the one which is either immediately above or immediately below the centre batten running along the turn of the bilge, and that the final closing plank will be the one nearest the midship frame in this strake.

The two lowest belts in the ship, those from the keel up, are the ones in which stealers are most likely to be needed, so I had better say something about them before you get too far with fitting this first belt from the keel. In fixing the planking battens we ran them with a view to getting a

natural run for the strakes across the face of the frames, and also to produce pleasing curves in the finished job. This however will not necessarily mean that battens spaced equidistant on the midship frame will be so
spaced at the stern, or for that matter the stem, although the difference
there is rarely sufficient to call for stealers. It is in the after end of the ship
between the keel and the underside of the counter that the effect of
unequal spacing is most likely to be noticed, for if the planks are to run
easily and naturally along the turn of the bilge, their after ends will tend to
sweep up under the bulge of the run, so opening out fan-wise as they
approach the stern-post, and it is to make up for this local expansion in
surface area that stealers have to be fitted. In a sailing model where scale
appearance is not important one could of course cut these strakes from
wider material, as in fact is often done in full-size yacht practice today, but
with the big wooden merchant ship there were factors which made this
impracticable. For such ships the planks might have to open out to two or
even three feet wide to make up the area required, and while such timber
would no doubt be available, it would be most difficult to work. In a ship of
large size it would be anything up to six inches thick and certainly not less
than three inches, and this not only has to be bent to the horizontal curve
and twist of the strake itself, but also the hollow curve of the frame in a
vertical direction. Ubviously two planks of say 12 in. wide can be worked
into these hollow curves more easily than a single one of say 24 in., and
so, short stealers were used to expand the ends of the strakes at these
points. This type of stealer is illustration *Sketch No.* 49 which shows two
ways of making it, in one it is half-checked into one of the adjoining
strakes, and in the other, quarter-checked into the plank on either side,
although the result is the same in either case, two strakes are increased
to three at the stern-post. Another form of stealer is used when the width
of the planking contracts to a point where, if carried out to the end, there
would not be room for adequate fastenings, and this is shown in the
Sketch No. 50. This type however is rarely necessary except perhaps in
some very bluff, round, apple-bowed craft.

The question of whether stealers will or will not be required will be
seen at a glance when spacing out the planks on the frames. Now let us
assume that having measured from keel to first batten above it on the midship frame, we find that there is room for seven strakes, and that on making the same check at the stern-post we find that six or six and a half of
the maximum accepted width will do, then obviously there will be no need
for stealers, but should the measurement up the stern-post show that
eight or eight and a half are required between keel and the first batten,
then stealers will have to be fitted. Had the difference been only a matter
of say half a strake, then we could have stretched the point and widened
the ends of all seven planks a shade to make up the required amount, but

more than that would look wrong.

Each stealer fitted will account for one additional plank, and here again, if only a plank and a fraction are required to make up the space, then we can make the end of the stealer a little wider than standard to cover this, but if one and a half planks are needed, then two stealers should be used, arranged with at least one unbroken strake between them. The shape of the hull will decide the length of the stealers, and this can be found by checking each frame until you reach the point where it again requires the full width of the strakes to cover the space between keel and batten, and this will be the one on which the stealer should in theory start, although in practice it is better to move back a couple of frames, and so make the "opening out" a little more easy. I have just said that one works from the frame which "again" requires the full width of the strakes, this is because the strakes will most probably have narrowed down for the first few frames from midships, then started to open out again, until they are back at the width they were midships, and as we have already seen would continue, but for the stealers, to open out until they were wider than midships, but I will deal with this contracting and expanding a little later.

Cutting and fitting the stealers is really quite simple, and as a first example we will take the one half-checked into one plank only, *Sketch No. 49A*. Having decided in which strake you are going to insert the stealer, probably in the centre of the belt if only one is required, while if there are more than one to go in, then the need for complete strakes between them will probably leave little choice. Make and fit the strake into which the stealer is to be inserted, carrying it its full breadth out to the stern, but do not glue or dowel it at this stage, instead mark out the top edge for the inset of the stealer, making the depth "U", *Sketch No. 51A*, half the width of the plank at that point, and the upper edge "Y" sweep up to the full width or whatever is required at the stern-post. This sweep should be similar in curvature to that of the lower edge of the plank, and when finished the after end of this plank will look as in the Sketch just referred to. Now take a short piece of full-width planking material and carefully cut its lower edge to fit into the "cut-out" portion of the plank just made, when these two match up perfectly the actual plank can be glued and dowelled in position, while the piece which is to make the stealer should be tacked in place with pins, as in *Sketch No. 51B*, as soon as the after edge has been made to fit the rabbet of the stern-post.

Now proceed to cut the next full plank, allowing the after end to override the uncut portion of the stealer and making the bottom edge sweep up to the top of the stealer at the stern-post. Run a sharp pencil along the bottom of this plank, then cut the stealer to this line, after which both plank and stealer can be glued and dowelled in place, and the remainder of the

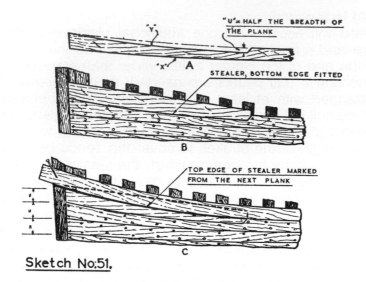

"U" = HALF THE BREADTH OF THE PLANK

STEALER, BOTTOM EDGE FITTED

TOP EDGE OF STEALER MARKED FROM THE NEXT PLANK

Sketch No. 51.

'A'.   PLANK ABOUT BILGE

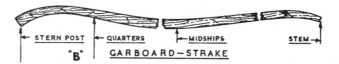

"B"   GARBOARD—STRAKE

NOTE: THE AMOUNT OF CURVATURE VARIES ACCORDING TO HULL FORM. THE CURVATURE ABOVE IS SLIGHTLY EXAGGERATED TO INDICATE GENERAL SHAPE.

Sketch No. 52.

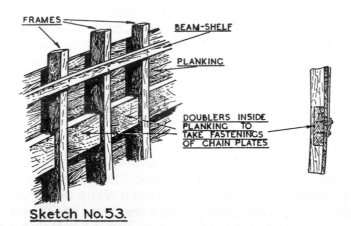

FRAMES

BEAM-SHELF

PLANKING

DOUBLERS INSIDE PLANKING TO TAKE FASTENINGS OF CHAIN PLATES

Sketch No. 53.

1/15

planking continued as before. The quarter-checked stealers will be made in the same way, except that the lower edge of the upper plank will also be cut out and the stealer marked off from it. With this type of stealer the depth "U" in both upper and lower planks will of course be only one quarter the width of each plank at this point. The widths of the after ends of both planks and stealer will be arrived at in the usual way, the number of planks along the stern-post being the same as on the midship section, plus one for every stealer to be fitted.

We will assume that you have gone ahead with the planking, doing alternative belts, first below the wale and then above the keel, until only the strake along the turn of the bilge remains. This too is worked from either end, and the last plank to go in will be that midships, a plank which you will probably find is dead straight and without any taper. This plank will have fixed planks on all four sides of it, and at first may look rather difficult to fit, but if you drive a couple of pins into it to act as "handles" for pushing it into place, you will find that it will slip into position like the last piece of a puzzle. So far I have assumed that you intend to have the model fully planked, but should you decide to do as I did and leave off a few strakes on one side, do not simply omit them and leave it at that, for if you do the rest of the planking on that side is likely to run out of truth. It is much better to fully plank the hull, but having decided just what planks you are going to leave off, merely tack these in place with small pins, so that they may be pulled off later without damage to the frames. They will come in handy anyway, for they will be used for just what they are, the "old planks" removed from the hull and left on the "ground" alongside the berth.

That brings us to the end of the planking of this particular model except for the bulwarks, which will not go on for a little time yet, for the next job will be to fit inside the hull sundry doublers for the rigging, etc., but before going on with that I think I had better say something about planking in general, more perhaps as it may effect the non-scale model. In models built for sailing and powered work the planking will not be laid in scale lengths, but each strake will be fitted in one piece where possible and the longest lengths workable where not. Even for this class of model I would still advise builders to make all strakes which have to fit into a rabbet at either end, in two or even three pieces. It can be extremely difficult to cut exactly a strake which will run right round the hull from bow to stern and yet fit perfectly into a rabbet at either end, I have tried it and that was my own experience, those two ends are usually at an angle to the edge of the plank, and have to be tucked into the shoulder of the rabbet. If made the least bit too long they will not make proper contact with the frames, while if a little too much is taken off, then they leave an ugly gap at the rabbet.

If I were building a working model I would lay all strakes in three planks, fitting the bow and stern first, then lastly a closing plank in the centre, which would have square butt ends easy to fit. In the topsides of course, assuming that the vessel has a transom stern, then a single strake fore and aft is quite workable, for the stem and can be fixed first, then working aft with sufficient length for the plank to overhang the transom, where it can be cut off flush after the fastening has been completed. There is another point in favour of the shorter plank however, even in a working model, and that is the curvature required at certain places in the hull. I have already mentioned that in the stern of any vessel the planks will often get narrower as they move aft from midships until they reach a point about two-thirds of the way to the stern, after which they will start to open out again, so that if put on in a single plank their shape would be rather like that in *Sketch No. 52A.* This is due to the fact that in a normal sailing ship hull the skin-girth on frames about two-thirds of the distance from midships to the stern, is much less than in any other part of the hull, except perhaps at the rabbet of the stem, and so the strakes have to narrow down to get through this bottle-neck, opening-up again as soon as they are clear of it. This effect is all the more marked because it all takes place below the turn of the run—the up-sweeping of the bilge into the counter—while above this level the taper is more or less constant from midships in either direction. The planks in the topsides will have considerable curvature in following the sweep of the sheer, and this is one objection to making even these in single lengths, for it means that they have to be cut out of fairly wide material to allow for this. The garboard strake will also require wide material if one tries to make it in one, for it usually forms a double "S" curve as in *Sketch No. 52B.*

Now let us return to *Leon.* A rather unusual feature of this vessel is the use of hawse-pipes for the anchor cable, the more general arrangement in small ships of her class, and for that matter most sailing vessels irrespective of size, was to fit hawse-holes in the bulwarks of small ships and in the bows below the to'gallant fo'castle in larger ones, the cable leading straight from these holes to the windlass. However in our case hawse-pipes have to be fitted and we must make provision for them before the deck goes on, otherwise it will not be possible to make a proper job. Carefully set out on the outside of the hull the exact centre of the hawse-pipe, checking that the two sides really are the same, for it would look very odd if when seen from the bow, one side turned out to be higher than the other. These pipes fall between the first and second cant-frames reading from the bow (E and D respectively on the Constructional Plan) and will actually cut slightly into the heel of the latter, but this will not matter since the planking will be reinforced by a doubler, which is what we have to fit at the moment.

Having marked the external centres of the hawse-pipes, drill a 1/16 in. hole square through the planking at this point, just to mark its position inside the hull. Now cut a piece of 1/8 in. thick material, sycamore if possible, about 5/8 in. long and wide enough to be a push fit between the two cant-frames then carefully hollow out one face so that it will sit in close contact with the planking directly over the hole you have drilled. It is important that this doubler should be a good close fit on the inside of the planking, since the hole for the hawse-pipe will probably cut right through at least one plank, and apart from forming the anchorage for the pipe, this block must keep the ends of the planks in position. When satisfied with the fit against the planking, glue this doubler in place, taking care that it is placed squarely over the l/16 in. hole, then fit a similar doubler on the other side of the ship. Pencil the actual size of the hawse-pipe round the hole, and if it does cut right through any of the planks, or even three-parts through, then it is as well to dowel them to the doubler on either side of the finished pipe. The actual drilling of the hole to take the brass pipe will be left until later.

The chain-plates, or metal straps, which attach the lower ends of the standing rigging to the hull, extend some distance down the sides, and it will be necessary to provide a suitable anchorage for their lower ends. The positions of the lower ends of these chain-plates can be obtained from the Sail and Rigging plan and should now be marked roughly on the hull. You do not need their exact positions at this stage, only the frames between or on which they are likely to fall. Having found this proceed to glue in a set of doublers between all frames effected, for both fore and main rigging, as shown in *Sketch No.* 53. These doublers should be about l/8 in. thick and l/2 in. deep, and like those for the hawse-holes should make proper contact with the planking. Their distance below the beam shelf will be obtained from the plans. All that matters is that the two pins which fix the lower ends of the chain-plates shall have something firm to go into. There is no need to dowel these doublers, for the chain-plate pins will serve that purpose.

The final job will be to fit the mast-steps on top of the keelson, although here I rather slipped up, for it would have been much easier to have fitted them to the keelson before the latter went into place. On the other hand the steps would have added difficulty in dowelling the keelson to the frames and keel, so perhaps it is a case of gaining on the roundabouts what one may have lost on the swings. In full-size practice the mortice in the mast-step would be cut square to match the square tennon on the heel of the mast, and of course they should be so made in the model, but I admit that in this case I used round holes, not because there was any difficulty on filing them out square, but I know from past experience how easy it is to cut the square tennon in the heel of the mast a shade out of truth with the square of the head, so that the latter had either to look slightly to port or starboard, or the nicely cut heel-tennon had to be "eased" a little to allow the mast to be squared up again, so I decided to use a round tennon and a drilled hole in the step. The step is made from a bit of 1/8 in. x l/4 in. sycamore about 5/8 in. long, with a 1/8 in. hole drilled in the centre. Remember to drill this hole at the same angle as the rake of the particular mast for which the step is intended. Carefully locate the centre of the mast on the keelson by measuring from adjacent frame centres, and mark it either with a small centre-punch hole or the point of a sharp pencil. Drill a hole in either end of the step and countersink them to take fine brass screws, then apply some glue to the underside of the step and after locating the mast tennon hole over your mark on the keelson, leave for the glue to dry, and when satisfied that it has set, drill the holes in the keelson for the brass screws and drive them home, so that your finished step will look as *Sketch No.* 54. You cannot be too careful about the location of the mast steps, for there will be no chance of adjusting them when once the deck is on, and on them will depend the rake of the masts in the finished ship. Another rather obvious point, although one only too easy to overlook, watch that the slope of the hole in the step is facing the right way when glueing down, it is very easy to turn the step round when applying the glue, and the angle of the hole is very slight and not easily noticed.

That now concludes the internal work on the hull, the next job being to fix the deck beams, but before doing this it is as well to give the interior whatever treatment it is intended to have, since this is more easily applied before the beams go in than after. My own method is very simple, I merely give the inside several coats of varnish, while in the ends where the planks are too close for the brush to get in, I just flood in thin varnish to fill up to where the brush can reach, giving it plenty of time to harden. In sailing models I cut strips of linen equal in width to the space between the frames, and while the first coat of varnish is still wet press these strips well into it from keelson to deck, using the handle of an old spoon to press the material home until the varnish is forced out through it. It is then left to dry, and finally given two more coats on top. Such a hull will never open up no matter how often it is alternatively in the water or left dry on a stand, and I would now apply the same treatment to showcase models, too, for they perhaps are most likely to be subject to dry over heated atmosphere, although none of my models which have merely been well varnished inside have shown any signs of opening up, but I have a 1/4 in. scale plank-built model which was originally intended for a showcase but never finished, which is showing the effects of plank shrinkage. This however is to be expected in this case for this hull was built over 30 years ago for demonstration purposes, and as I was working very much against time, it did not have even one coat of varnish either inside or out. For thirty odd years that model has just "kicked about" on sundry tables, below benches, and in the sun on window sills, without anything to protect the bare wood, so it is not surprising that its seams are opening up a little and the end of an odd deck plank is needing re-fixing. If this model had been varnished and linen coated inside I think it would have been as good today as when first built, even though the outside was still without any treatment. It is still not completely beyond repair, for if I sink it in one of the large print-washing baths for a week-end, it takes up again, and if the deck were torn out and the inside properly treated, it would probably "stay put". One reason why it was never finished was the fact that I could never have been happy about it knowing that inside the wood was bare, so it has now been "written off" these many years.

I mention this old model to illustrate the importance of properly treating a plank-on-frame model to preserve the wood, particularly inside. The material from which this class of model is built is very light, and therefore more subject to atmospherical changes, so it is well worth while taking the time to see that the inside has several good coats of varnish before the deck goes on, and on this point I think three coats of fairly thin varnish much better than two heavy ones. It will take longer of course, because one coat must not only be dry, but also set hard before the next goes on. Of course the inside could be painted, but I think paint more apt to crack should the planks tend to shrink whereas varnish always seems to retain some elasticity. If the joints between any of your planks are not as tight as they ought to be, thin varnish will find them out and probably come out through the seam, but this is all to the good, for *if* you have any such seams, then the varnish will caulk them and any that finds its way on to the outer surface can be scraped off when it is dry. The second and third coats will not come through. However there ought not to be any joints through which even the first coat can find its way.

If your model is to be built with all the frames exposed and only planked down to say the waterline, then it would be as well to French polish the keelson, frames, deadwood, etc., before fitting, leaving bare only just those small faces which have to be glued and dowelled to other components, or have others fixed to them, just as we will be varnishing the undersides of the deckbeams before we fit them, since it would be very difficult to do so after they are in position.

CHAPTER IV

PLANKING THE DECK AND BULLWARKS

WHEN the varnish, or whatever internal treatment has been used, has had time to dry, the deck beams can be taken in hand, but the first job will be to make a template for the "rise of beam", which of course is the camber of the deck. This rise is 1/4 in. per foot, or in other words, for every foot of length the centre of a beam will rise 1/4 in. above the sides, and as this is constant throughout the ship, one template will do for all beams, irrespective of their individual lengths. For example, if the midship beam of a model is 12 in. long, then the centre of that beam will be l/4 in. above the sides, but nearer the bow where a beam may be 6 in. long, then its centre will be 1/8 in. above the sides, a proportion which will apply throughout the model.

The template should be made of cardboard or very thin plywood, and a little longer than the longest beam in the ship. It simplifies matters to work in multiples or parts of a foot, so we will make the base of our template 6 in. long. Take a piece of cardboard or plywood and rule a straight line; mark the centre of this and then set off points 3 in. on either side. At the centre point draw a short vertical and mark off 1/8 in. above the base, then take a flexible straight edge and bend it so that it touches the three points obtained, and while holding it there get someone to run a sharp pencil round it, so that the result will be as *Sketch No. 55*. Carefully cut to the curved line and you will have a template for the top of every beam in the ship.

In the *Leon* model all beams extend across the faces of the frames and butt against the inside of the wale, but this will not be the case in all vessels, and there is no reason why they should not butt on the frame, or have some butting against the frames and others between frames. The advantage of the method used in this model is that it provides a very strong fixing even though the beams are not installed until after the model is fully planked, as in the present case. The beams for the model are 3/32 in. sided and 3/16 in. moulded, and should be cut from either 3/8 in. x 1/8 in. or 5/16 in. x 1/8 in. to allow for cleaning up and the rise of beam.

Beams which fall in way of hatches or mast-partners do not run right across the ship, but end in the fore-and-aft carlings, but in the first

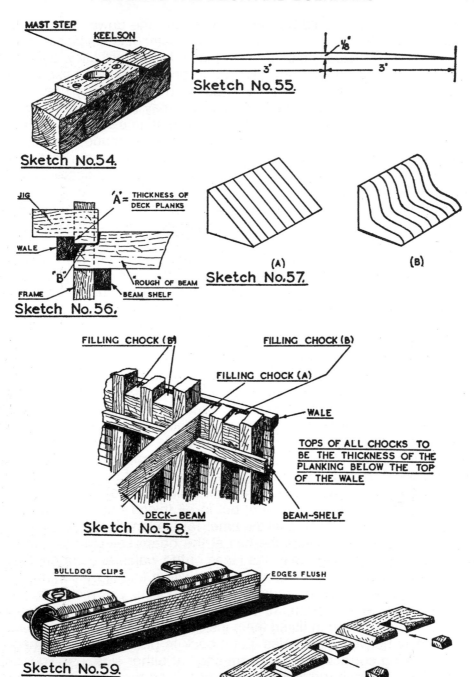

MAST STEP

KEELSON

Sketch No.54.

⅛"

3"   3"

Sketch No.55.

JIG

"A" = THICKNESS OF DECK PLANKS

WALE

"B"

FRAME

"ROUGH" OF BEAM

BEAM SHELF

Sketch No.56.

(A)

(B)

Sketch No.57.

FILLING CHOCK (B)   FILLING CHOCK (B)

FILLING CHOCK (A)

WALE

TOPS OF ALL CHOCKS TO
BE THE THICKNESS OF THE
PLANKING BELOW THE TOP
OF THE WALE

DECK—BEAM   BEAM—SHELF

Sketch No.58.

BULLDOG CLIPS   EDGES FLUSH

Sketch No.59.

FILLING-PIECES

Sketch No.60.

instance all beams should be made full length, the unwanted centres of those in way of hatches, etc., being cut away later. It is advisable to make all beams before actually fitting any in place, for this will allow them to be given two coats of varnish and allowed to dry before being fixed, but do not forget to mark each one as it is made and so avoid any possibility of getting one in the wrong place later on. This may seem a very unnecessary precaution, but near the centre of the ship beams are very much alike and much time will be saved by numbering them as made; further, make a point of numbering them all in the same place, say the port side aft, so that the figure will not only identify the beam, but also indicate its fore or after face. Near midships the ends of the beams will be almost square and their tops nearly flat, but nearer the ends of the ship the tops of the beams will slope to the sheer of the deck, while the ends will have to be cut to the angle of the wale.

The beams could of course be varnished in position, but it would be very difficult, if not almost impossible, to do this really well, and I regard the covering of all internal woodwork as being a matter of the greatest importance if the model is to last. There is no reason why a well-built model should not last several generations, particularly if reasonable precautions are taken during construction, so a little extra time spent in this direction is well worth while.

There is one more simple jig which is worth making before we start cutting out the beams, and that is as illustrated in *Sketch No.* 56. Its use will be clear, the "step" marked "A" is equal to the thickness of planking being used in the deck, so that when the roughly cut beam is placed in position, a fine pencil run along the under side of the jig "B", marks the depth of the beam at the ends, and from these marks the rise-of-beam template will draw in the top cutting line. However let us start making one of the beams midships, it does not matter which, for we are going to make them all before fixing any of them, but in all things I usually like to start midships and work outwards all the time. Take a length of the 3/8 in. x 1/8 in. material and lay it across the hull at the beam selected for the start, mark the width between the inside faces of the wales and cut off, leaving it just a shade full to allow a final dressing with a fine file. About midships the ends will of course be roughly square, but as you move out in the directions of bow and stern, so will the angle of the ends increase and more care be required in fitting them inside the wales. When the material will fit nicely between the wales, put it back in place, and after checking that it is sitting correctly on the beam-shelf at either side, use your small jig to mark the depth required at either end, also mark the lower edge at the points where it meets the beam-shelf on either side, for it is from these points, and not the ends, that the curve of the underside of the beam will run.

Take the spar out of the hull, and with your rise-of-beam template strike in the curve between the points representing the depth of the beams at the ends, and with the same template strike in the curve of the underside between the two marks representing the faces of the beam-shelves after which the beam can be cut out and laid aside for varnishing later. If your model is to be fully planked there is of course no real reason why the underside of the beam should be curved, that is a matter of taste and it will not be seen either way when the model is completed, but for all the extra work involved, the properly curved beam is much more pleasing to the eye during the final stages of construction, it looks more "ship-shape", and if your pleasure is largely gained from the work of building, that is important. Personally I always like to see something as near as possible to the real thing, even during construction, which is why I so favour the "built" model. To me the pleasure of model work is two-fold that of actually making the various components, and the sight of such components, either partly made or completely finished, but that is purely a personal viewpoint.

The beam just made is one near the centre of the ship, and at that point the top will probably be flat, but further fore or aft the tops of all beams will have to be made to slope to the true sheer of the hull, otherwise the planking would make contact only with one corner of the beam, and so prove "springy" and difficult when you come to dowel it in place, to say nothing of being a very poor job. Fixing this slope on the top of the beam is not difficult however. When you put your roughly cut beam back into the hull for marking the depth of the ends with the small jig, you can add the angle of slope at the same time. After you have marked the depth on the timber, raise it until these marks are level with the top of the wales on either side, then run a sharp pencil point along the top of the wale, and the required angle will be shown on the end of the beam, then when cutting out the top curve make the cut sufficiently wide to allow this slope to be put on with a chisel. There is another point to be remembered about these beams towards the ends of the ship, and that is that the undersides of the beams have to be given the same slope as the tops, since the beam-shelf also runs up at these points, and unless the bottom of the beam is sloped accordingly, only one edge will make contact with the shelf. Do not forget that the bevel on the underside must be put on *before* the ends of the beam are measured for depth. In a small scale model these differences will probably be very slight—but still important—but in a larger model failure to cut them properly can give a lot of trouble at a later stage by allowing beams to get slightly out of line of sheer, so that when one comes to plank them one has to start trimming down or fitting very thin "shims" of wood to build them up. So once more the oft repeated warning, do not pass anything which is not quite right, for if you do it will bring you plenty of trouble at a later date. No great skill is required in any of this work, merely great care and attention to small detail.

When all the beams are made they should be given two or three coats of thin varnish, but leaving bare their tops which will be in contact with the deck planking, and their extreme ends which will be glued to frames and filling chocks. Those beams which form the fore or after ends of hatches, etc. should also be left bare over those portions which will be inside the openings of the hatches and such like, for to these faces the coamings will later be glued. A number of lodging-knees will be required at various points of contact between the beams and carlings, mast-partners, etc., while in full size practice many such knees would also be required between the beams and the ship's side, as will be seen in the Construction Plan of the Zulu *Plate No.* 6, but they have not been included in the *Leon* model where the beams will be fully anchored by means of chocks, which will be described later. However a certain number of these knees are required, and they can be made while the beams are being varnished and allowed to dry. The making of these knees is one of the few jobs on which we can apply mass-production methods, and there are two ways of doing this, one may either make a number of small triangles of hardwood and clamp them together as in *Sketch No.* 57A, then file them to shape as in "B", or alternatively one may take a strip of hardwood and shape it as a single piece to that shown in "B", sawing off "slices" as required to form the knees. If the latter method is used then the wood must be either Box, Sycamore or some similar type which has scarcely any grain, since the latter will of course be running the wrong way through the finished knee. The other alternative is to make them in smaller numbers by cutting the triangular block out of a piece of say 1 in. or 1¼ in. material in which the grain can be arranged to run properly. However, make a number of these knees and varnish them, all except the faces which will be in contact with beams and carlings, etc., and put them aside until needed.

Assuming that our beams can now be handled, we will get them into the ship, starting with that fitted to *Frame No.* 11. This beam forms the forward end of the main hatch, so on its after face mark and cut the mortices to receive the ends of the carlings, then put the beam in place and hold it to its frame either with small clamps or temporary wedges to the next frame. Leave that beam in place and move aft to the next full beam, the one which will form the after end of the hatch; mark and cut the carling mortices on the fore side of this and fit as before, again holding it by means of clamps or wedges. Now take two pieces of the material used for making the beams, and on these mark the length of the carlings, including that to go into the mortices at either end, cut them a shade long and then reduce their depth to that of the beams. Carefully fit these carlings in place, filing down the ends until they are a tight fit without forcing the beams out of line. Now take up the beam which is to form the two half-beams between those just made, lay it across the model in its correct position and mark each carling at the points where this beam crosses them, also mark the beam where it will require to be cut, not forgetting the depth of the mortice to be cut in the carling. Remove the carlings and cut the mortices, then cut the beam, slightly full to allow for final fitting, and fit the two half-beams so that they are a good fit between the inside of the wale and the mortices in the carlings, but without forcing the latter out of the straight. When satisfied with all these joints, remove the carlings and half-beams—leaving the two main beams in position—and after smearing the ends of the carlings with glue, put them back in place. Glue the inboard ends of the half-beams—not the outer ends—and fit them into the carlings, then fix the outer ends to their frame with clamps or wedges and leave for the glue to dry.

When the glue is dry, remove the clamps or wedges from the ends of the beams and lift out the complete assembly, then drill through the beams into the ends of the carlings and dowel them. Do the same through the carlings into the ends of the half-beams, although in this case you wlll have to drill down at a slight angle and skew-dowel them, since the width of the hatch will not be sufficient to allow you to drill horizontally. These dowels will probably come out on the under side of the half-beams, but that does not matter, they will be cut off flush. Next glue and dowel the lodging knees in the angles as shown on the plans, and when this is dry, varnish the exposed portions of the carlings, all except that forming the inside of the hatch. When the varnish is dry, replace the assembly in the hull, having first applied glue to all faces of the ends of all beams. While the glue is still wet make and fix the filling-chocks (A) as shown in *Sketch No.* 58. These chocks, as their name suggests, fill the space between the face of the beam and the next frame, with their tops flush with the top of the beam, and their lower edges down at beam-shelf level, or longer if you wish. They are glued to the beam on one side, the frame on the other, while the other face is glued to the inside of the planking. The important points are that the chocks shall be a good fit and so lock the beams in position, and secondly that their upper surfaces shall be the thickness of the deck planking below the top of the wale.

The rest of the beams are fitted in the same way except that some, as shown on the plan, have doublers or packers inside the hatch openings to reduce the area. In full-size practice these beams would be placed exact-ly on the line of the hatch, but that would mean they would land on the inner face of a frame, which of course is quite in order, but in the model it was considered better to sacrifice this minor point of detail for the advan-tage of the stronger fixing obtained by allowing the beam to cross the face of the frame. The beams are fitted into the mast partners as shown on Construction Plan. In my own model I actually dowelled the beams to the frames before fitting the filling-chocks, but that was merely because I like the work, it adds very little, if anything, to the strength of the finished job, since the beams are completely locked by the chocks. When all beams are in, the exposed surfaces of the chocks, except the top should be varnished.

So far I have only mentioned filling-chocks between beams and adjacent frames, but I also fit them between all frames, whether there are beams or not, so that there is a solid belt of timber running right round the hull at deck level and made up of chocks, frames, beams, wale and beamshelf, as shown in *Sketch No. 58B.* This is purely optional and I have not shown it on the Construction Plan, but the strength of such a hull is amazing, I believe that turned on its side one could stand on it without fear of crushing it, and I regard it as being well worth the trouble involved— which is not very much. I know that one does not build models to stand on them, and for that reason I have not included these chocks as part of the original design, instead I have shown each beam skew-dowelled to the adjacent frame, and that together with the fact that the beams run out to the inside of the wale, will produce a model amply strong for all practical purposes, but for myself, I like the use of filling-chocks, which incidentally were common practice in many yards building small vessels for coastal work or fishing, vessels which were in frequent contact with quay walls, or being jostled one with the other when forcing their way into the fleet crowded round the fish-dock.

To some model builders all this structural work below deck may appear a waste of time in view of the fact that it is to be completely covered by planking and not seen again, but one must remember that such constructional work in the real ship was not put there because people going below would see it, it was there because the strength of the ship depended upon it, and for that same reason it is not a waste of time to fit an adequate number of beams and frames in a model, quite apart from the point mentioned earlier in this book, the effect it has on the external finish if the model is to be French polished or varnished. Further, if the builder intends to leave off a few planks here and there from the ship's side, there is no reason why he should not do the same with the deck, in which case the deck beams would be exposed in places. There is nothing out of the ordinary in a vessel in shipyard hands having a few planks missing from the deck, in fact many wooden ships had at least one or two completely new decks in their lifetime, while the replacement of those sections which got a lot of wear, either in handling the ship or working cargo, was common indeed, so if you do not like the idea of covering all the work put into the deck beams, then let the deck be "under repair" and leave off a few planks, there will be nothing odd about this. Perhaps I am something of a crank on this subject, but I have always preferred "atmosphere" to polish, and I would rather model an old ship under repair than one all "bright and shining" on a stand. We now have the hull fully framed except for the quarterdeck beams and the three short ones below the anchor-deck forward, so the laying of the maindeck can be taken in hand, but make certain that the model is well supported by wedges under the bilge, since it *must* be stiff for this job, for if it wobbles about or shakes on its jig the probable result will be a drill broken off in a beam. At this stage I still had the extensions on the fore and after ends of the keel, in fact the model was still in its original jig, but there is no reason why it should be, providing it is well supported.

The deck planking is not as wide as that used in the ship's sides, and for this model I used 3/32 in. x l/16 in. material. The deck could be thicker of course providing suitable allowance is made in the level of the deck beams. In larger working models there is no real objection to laying a 1/16 in. plywood deck on top of the beams and then running your deck planks on top of this, but if this method is used there are several points to be kept in mind, firstly to make allowance for it on top of the beams, secondly to see that there are plenty of strong points in the hull to which the plywood can be screwed down with fairly strong screws, for as I will mention later there is a lot of strain in such a deck. Lastly, remember to see that the centres of all beams are drawn on the upper side of the plywood, so that the planks can be dowelled into the beams and the line of the dowels across the deck appear in the correct places. In small and showcase models however, I do not consider this method satisfactory, and it is far better to lay the planking directly on the beams. It is expecting too much of plywood, even very thin stuff, to bend to the sweep of the sheer in one direction and the camber of the deck at right angles to it, unless one can get plenty of screws to hold it down, and these will come in the way of the dowels for the planking. Further, if you intend to fit proper open hatches, you will find that as soon as you cut these openings in the plywood, it will tend to fold across at the narrow side decks rather than follow the true sweep of the sheer.

We will assume that the planks are to be laid directly on the beams but before we start work, there is one little tip which the late Dr. Longridge gave me in the early twenties, when he was building his famous model of the *Cutty Sark*, and which I have found well worth following. When you have your lengths of planking material cut to the required breadth, get a few sheets of black paper such as is used for wrapping photographical materials, then take a small pile of planks, and after lining them up, hold them in a pair of clamps, *Sketch No.* 59, then glue them along one edge and place them face down on a sheet of the black paper, finally putting some weights on top and leaving them to dry. When the glue has set run a razor blade down between each plank, which will then come away with a strip of black paper, the thickness of the plank, all along one edge. When the planks are laid "black and plain" edges together, the general effect will be that of a properly caulked deck.

Dr. A. K. Tulloch of Dundee, whose work on power craft models will be mentioned in greater detail in Vol. II., puts forward another method, which he has proved to be very successful, and that is to mix Reeves black watercolour with cold water glue, which is run along the edge of the plank before fixing.

However to return to the work in hand, cut your planks into lengths of about 2½ in. or 3 in., which represents the maximum likely to be found in the real ship, then start on the centreline of the ship, although here, thanks to the various hatches, companions, etc., there will be no full length planks. The greatest distance is between the fore and main hatches, but as most of this area will be covered by the deck-house, there is no harm in running these planks right through without bothering about the placing of the butts. As usual I start midships, so take the first length of plank, and lay one end against the inner edge of the beam forming the after end of the main hatch, then with a pencil mark on the other the curve of the mast-hole in the partners and cut the plank to this. Hold this plank in a pair of fine tweezers and coat the underside with fairly thick varnish lay the plank back in position and proceed to dowel it to each beam and the mast partners, across which lines should have been pencilled indicating the line of the beams. Incidentally mention of the partners reminds me of another point regarding these. I find it a good thing to make the holes in these larger than actually required for the mast, so that the final adjustment for rake and thwartship plumb can be made by means of wedges as in full-size practice and as will be described in Vol. II. when dealing with stepping the masts.

Continue laying the centre plank the full length of the ship, then lay the one on either side of it, also running the full length, and so on, always working out from the centre, and of course always laying the planks "plain edge to papered". In this way you will be certain that when you arrive at the outer edges of the hatches you will not find that you have a full plank running up one side and only a three-quarters wide plank up the other.

Before your centre planks reach the bow, you will have to fit the pawl-bitt, a post with its heel in the deadwood and fixed on the after side of the beam at frame No. 3, small blocks of 1/8 in. square material will have to be fixed on three sides of this post at the level of the deck beam to take the ends of the planks which end there or have to be fitted round the post.

When you get outside the width of the hatches you will have to watch the placing of the butts, working on the same rule as already described for

Fig. 13
PLANKING-BATTENS IN USE.

Fig. 14.
This model was planked upside down:
Note use of special spring clamps.

1/8 in. SCALE MODEL OF *LEON*
By Professor Favez.

Fig. 15.
Windlass and Forestay.

Fig. 16.
Dead-eyes and Chain-plates.

the side planking and illustrated in *Sketch No.* 40, but as you are working out from the centre all the time, you will only require to settle the butts on one side, since the planks on the other will be the same. Continue in this way until you start to meet the sides of the ship, where the planks should be carried out to the inner face of the wale, being fitted round the bulwark stanchions as necessary and having their ends dowelled to the filling-chocks. In a full-size ship there would be a margin plank right round inside the bulwarks, and into this the ends of the deck planks would be joggled, but as in *Leon* the wide covering-board completely hid the margin plank, it was not fitted in the model.

The next item to go on will be the covering-board, which may be described briefly as a board which covers the joint between the deck and the hull proper, and in the construction used in the case of *Leon* this is literally true, although more generally it covers the joint between the waterway and the ship's side, but I say more about these alternative arrangements later. Another point which differs in different ships is the construction of the bulwark stanchions, and this will naturally effect the covering-board. I have already mentioned that the most common arrangement was for the bulwark stanchion to be a separate unit fitted between the frames and extending for a short distance down inside the hull, in which case the covering board is put on full breadth with square holes cut in it through which the stanchions are inserted. Other ships, and the *Leon* model is one example, have the stanchions made as part of the actual frames or timbers, and therefore the covering-board has to be fitted round them, and this is what we have to do with our model.

However before fitting this board the surface of the deck can be cleaned down, and at this stage you will appreciate the fact that you have not so far fitted the hatch coamings or any other projections above the deck other than the pawl-bitt, which had to go in owing to its fixing to the deadwood and deck beam. If the edge of any of the planks appears to ride a shade high alongside its neighbour, due perhaps to some slight inequality in thickness, as will often happen in material purchased to pre-cut dimensions, then it can be scraped down with a razor blade, or part of a blade, after which the whole surface should be cleaned up with the finest sandpaper and later given one or two coats of French polish, as a preservative and not to produce a high gloss. The highly polished type of deck may look all right in the large "Shipping Office" type of model of a modern liner, but it is all wrong in a model of a small cargo sailing ship, where in fact such a deck would be a positive death-trap at sea. Why must we have all this high polish on so many models? It is completely unreal. Of course I know that I have not been entirely true to my convictions in my model of *Leon*, in that I did not paint her outside, but on the other hand neither have I polished her, the outside like the deck was given several coats of French polish, applied with a pad of course, but none of them worked up to a gloss, and as with the deck, applied merely as a preservative. The reason for not painting was that in this ship I wished to retain the full beauty of line only to be found in the flow of the planks along the sides of a wooden ship, and which with a really tightly planked hull would to a large extent be lost under even a very thin coat of paint. However I am getting ahead of my subject, for we are not nearly ready to consider the external treatment of the hull, which is still without bulwarks.

When the deck has been cleaned up we can start fitting the covering-board, and this is best put on in scale lengths, not only because this is true to type, but also because it is the best way to make a good job. It is one thing to fit this board round four or five fairly closely spaced stanchions, but an entirely different matter to put it on all in one piece and get a good fit all round all stanchions. I find it better to make a template of each section and cut a pair of boards—one for each side of the ship, from that after it has been fitted. So take a piece of thin cardboard about three inches long, and starting in the bow sketch in the outline as shown by the deck-line on the plans, and an inner line representing the inboard edge of the covering board. The finished breadth of this board in the *Leon* model is 1/4 in., but it will require to be cut out of much wider material to allow for the curvature and fitting, while the thickness will be 1/16 in. When in position the outer edge should be just inside the external face of the wale, on top of which it sits, as shown in the plans.

Having cut your card roughly to the shape of the finished covering-board—do not be too neat in the first cutting, particularly on the inboard edge for you want a little spare to play with—place it on the tops of the stanchions and mark the template with their positions, cut out the slots, then feed the template into place on deck a little at a time, cutting and fitting as necessary. These first bow sections can be a little tricky, so do not be surprised if, just when you think you have got it right, you find that you have cut a little too much off the card at some point or another. If you have, use that card to mark out another, correcting the points at fault then scrap it and start again. When once these curved sections are in, the rest of the work is simple. When satisfied with your template, both for fit round the stanchions and also for internal and external curves, you can use it for marking out two pieces of wood, but do not forget to first test your template on the opposite side just to make certain that the two sides of the ship are, as they should be, identical. If they are not then you will have to make two templates, while if they are, remember that the two sides will be opposite hands, therefore the template should be turned over when marking out the second piece. Of course the wood can be turned over, but it is possible that the grain on one side may be better looking than the other and you will wish to keep that side up in both pieces. I used some 1/16 in.

cedar for the covering-boards.

Arrange the joint with the next length to fall on the face of a frame if at all possible, since this will avoid an extra joint appearing on the outside of the hull. Use scarfed joints between sections, as shown in *Sketch No.* 60. When you have the first section cut out and carefully fitted round the stanchions, lift it, then glue the under side, and after replacing, dowel into the filling-chocks (through the deck planking of course). The inner and outer edges of the board will have their top corners rounded off as shown in the sketch referred to. When fitted there will of course be small sections missing on top of the wale where the board has been fitted round the stanchions, and bits of the same material will be glued into these so that the outer edge will be unbroken when completed. Make templates for each section in turn, and carry the covering-board the length of the ship, after which it should be French polished if that is to be the finish of the model, or painted if not. If it is French polished then it will have to be brush applied, since it will not be very convenient to use a pad round the stanchions.

Now that the covering-boards are on, this is a good stage at which to fit the three cavils, or large timber cleats, which are inside the bulwarks on each side. In this model these are from 3/32 in. square material, sycamore or box if possible, with the corners smoothed away in the portions outside the stanchions, so as to reduce chafe in the gear belayed to them. These cavils take the place of the bollards of larger or metal built vessels, and on them the mooring lines are made fast when in dock, while they also serve as cleats for some of the heavy running gear when at sea. The forward and the after cavils have two iron bars down through them, and the centre cavil, three. These bars serve as belaying pins, but unlike the proper pin, they are fixtures and cannot be lifted out of position. In the model they are made of short lengths of brass wire. When you have the six cavils made, polish or varnish them, then file this off the portions which will be in contact with the stanchions, put a spot of glue on these points then put the cavils in place on the stanchions, and dowel them from the outside, letting the dowels go right through, they can be cut off both sides later.

Now is a good time to fit the hawse-pipes, these I made from brass tube. First mark out on deck the point where they should come through, which as will be seen from the plans is opposite the centre of the windlass barrel port and starboard. At this point drill a 1/32 in. pilot hole then enlarge it to say 3/32 in. with the drill held as near as possible to the angle the finished pipe will take. Next, using the pilot hole already drilled in the side of the hull, drill a 3/32 in. hole upwards through the doubler fitted inside the hull, again keeping the drill as near as possible to the finished angle of the pipe. With a fine round warding file passed right through the ship's side and out on to the deck clean up the hole through the doubler, taking great care not to enlarge or damage the hole through the side planking. Now take a piece of 1/8 in. O.D. brass tube and carefully fit it in the hole and out on to the deck, mark on it the lines of both deck and ship's side, then cut it off so that it will project about 1/16 in. above the deck and 1/32 in. out from the ship's side. This 1/8 in diameter is really the outside diameter of the flange on the side of the ship, and therefore the 1/32 in. which the pipe projects from the side of the ship represents the thickness of the flange. It will now be clear why great care must be taken with the hole through the side of the hull, since there will be no real flange to cover any slight damage which might be done. Properly done this makes a much neater job than attempting to fit an oval flange on the outside of this pipe. The flange in the original ship is very small and any flange imposed on the brass tube would look out of scale, so it is better to allow the thickness of the brass tube to represent both pipe and external flange.

The pipe should be a push fit through the hole in the doubler inside the hull, but at the deck a little play in the hole is not so important, for here one can solder a small wire flange, or a deck plate as shown in the drawings. This end of the pipe cannot be seen when the small anchor deck is in position. The important matter in fitting these pipes is that the lower end be cut at the correct angle, and that it projects only 1/32 in. to represent the thickness of the flange. If you can get some brass tube of say 3/32 in. O.D. and with a very thin wall, then use that and fit a small flange of wire round the lower end, at the angle of the hull of course, then file this flat after soldering, but to have added a flange to the tube I had would have looked too heavy and out of scale, for as will be seen from the picture of this vessel which forms the frontispiece, the flanges in the ship herself were very light.

The beam-shelves for the quarterdeck and anchor-deck beams should now be fitted while it is possible to dowel them right through from the outside of the stanchions. These shelves should be arranged so that the deck planking in each case will finish flush with the top of the bulwark planking but below the bulwark capping-rail which will overlap the planking and act as covering-board. The method of fixing those beam-shelves is just as for those of the main deck.

Before starting the bulwark planking put in the eyes for the forestay, one in each knighthead as shown in *Sketch No. 61B*. These eyes should have a good thread, for you will probably put considerable strain on them when setting up the forestay, and if they should pull out when once the anchordeck has been laid, the only answer would be to rip it up again. As will be seen from the plans, in the original ship the forestay passes down through holes in the anchor deck and is set up to thimbles shackled to these eye-boats or eye-plates, *Sketch No. 61A*, and on that I will have

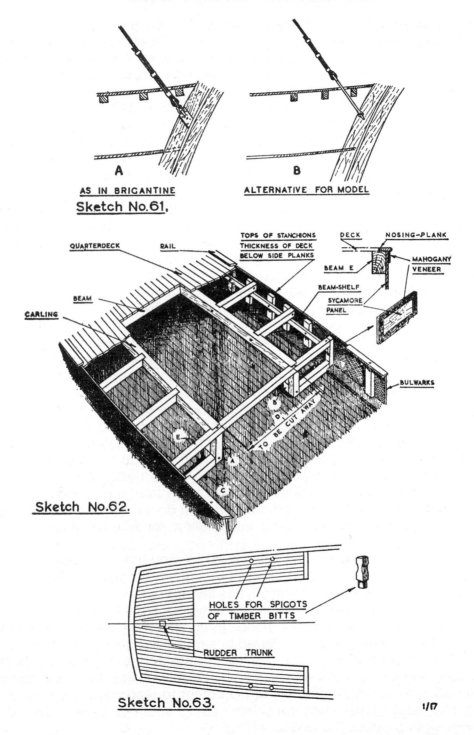

A
AS IN BRIGANTINE

B
ALTERNATIVE FOR MODEL

Sketch No.61.

QUARTERDECK

RAIL

TOPS OF STANCHIONS
THICKNESS OF DECK
BELOW SIDE PLANKS

DECK   NOSING-PLANK

BEAM E

MAHOGANY
VENEER

BEAM

BEAM-SHELF

SYCAMORE
PANEL

CARLING

BULWARKS

TO BE CUT AWAY

E

B
D

A

C

Sketch No.62.

HOLES FOR SPIGOTS
OF TIMBER BITTS

RUDDER TRUNK

Sketch No.63.

1/17

more to say in Vol. II., but it does serve to illustrate the need for planning out the sequence of work many moves ahead of that actually in progress. The setting up of the forestay is part of the rigging of the ship, which will not be taken in hand until after the bulwarks are on, anchor and quarter-decks laid, hatches and deck fittings made and fixed, houses built, and masts and spars made and stepped, etc. Yet thanks to the fact that in the full-size ship a man can crawl below the anchor deck and reach these eyes, whereas in the model they will be quite inaccessible when once the anchor-deck is in position, you will in fact have to do one or two items of rigging before you have finished planking the hull. This of course will not apply in all vessels, it is due to the particular arrangement of the forestay in this ship, but if this item does not arise in another ship, something else will, so the point I am trying to make is that one should always spend a little time working out an order of progress before making a start on any section of the work; always know just what you have to do next, several moves ahead of the particular job about to be tackled. It will take a little thought, but an hour or so spent in quiet contemplation of the work already done, and considering the jobs ahead, will in the long run save many hours later in trying to get at something which was within easy reach when you last thought about it, but which has since become almost inaccessible, or perhaps completely so. A little consideration can make all the difference to the ease in working. The mast steps could have been fitted after the beams were in, but it is much better to fit them before; the hatch coamings could have been fitted before the deck was planked, or as soon as the planking was finished, but cleaning and polishing the deck would have taken twice as long and probably not have been so well done, had its surface been broken up by these various projections. The cavils could be fitted after the bulwarks are planked, but it is much better to fit them first, since that will allow you to drill and dowel them from the outside instead of inside the bulwarks. So my advice is, do not do a single job without first having considered the work which has to follow, for time spent in this way is time well spent.

The bulwarks may now be taken in hand, and these in *Leon* follow a typically Scandinavian pattern, which by making the planking forward of the quarterdeck thinner than that aft, has the appearance of forming a hollow panel forward and a flush side aft, as will be seen from the picture of the ship and Professor Favez's model. In my own model I departed from this because I have alwalys preferred to see the line of the bulwarks carried right through to the stern, I think the sudden change to the flush planking rather spoils the look of the hull. I still think this, but I now regret that I allowed my dislike for this arrangement to lead me away from the true ship, and I have often considered fitting doubling strakes over the planks aft to produce the additional thickness.

The actual work of planking the bulwarks really needs no explanation, for it follows that of the hull, including the planking of alternate sides in stead of finishing one side first. The material for the main bulwarks forward of the quarterdeck should be 3/32 in. x 1/32 in., while that further aft will be 3/32 in. x 1/16 in. Start at the bow and run the first strake immediately above the covering-board, making each plank about 2½ in. or 3 in. long. When you reach the last butt *before* the point where the planks increase in thickness, cut the next plank from the 1/16 in. material. Hold this plank on the stanchions and mark where the change in thickness has to take place, then remove it again, and with a flat warding file reduce the thickness of the plank forward of this mark to 1/32 in., after which it can be glued and dowelled in place as are all the other planks. This may perhaps sound a rather round-about way to change the thickness of the planking at this point, but it is in fact the only satisfactory one. Obviously one cannot have a straight line of butts running all up the bulwarks, the joints in the planks must be arranged according to the rule, so this change of thickness can only be made by reducing that portion of each plank which projects into the bulwarks. From the after end of this plank the rest of the strake will of course be laid in 1/16 in. material.

When this first strake is on fore and aft, fit the same one on the opposite side of the ship, then; lay the second strake, again changing over to 1/16 in. material at the butt before the actual increase, and planking in this material right out to the stern. Incidentally, all strakes should be carried right out to the after face of the stern frame and finally finished off flush with it. Continue adding strakes until there is room only for a narrow one between that last fitted and the top of the stanchions, then run this last strake in 1/16 in. material throughout. As a matter of fact you will probably find that a length of 1/16 in. square stuff will do this job, but if the space to be filled exceeds this, then cut a few strips off the 3/32 in. x 1/16 in planks and finally dress them down flush with the tops of the stanchions. The bulwarks are now planked fore and aft, but we cannot finish them until both quarterdeck and anchor-deck are planked, since the rail on top of the bulwarks carries right round the ship and at the ends acts as covering board for the two raised decks.

However there is one more item of planking we can do before moving to these small decks, and that is to cover in the transom. This planking offers no difficulty, it runs in straight horizontal strakes right across the stern frame, or fashion-piece if that is the type of stern you have used. First of all cut out a 1/4 in. x 1/16 in. plank *"A"* in *Sketch No*. 47. The object of this is to act as a "covering-board" for the ends of the planking coming up under the counter, and the best way to make it is to use 1/4 in. wide material and cut the upper curve only, making the plank long enough to extend a fraction beyond the sides of the transom. When satisfied with the shape of the top of this plank, glue and dowel it along the bottom edge of the transom, on which it should rest 1/8 in. and overhang the planking below the counter as shown in the small section in *Sketch No.* 47. When the glue is dry carefully pare off the overhang with a sharp chisel and finally clean up so that the lower edge of this plank is at the same bevel and flush with the planks of the counter. When once this plank is on all that need be done is to fill the area above it with horizontal planks of the same thickness and allowing them to slightly overhang the ends. If you have used a solid fashion-piece instead of stern frames, do not forget to rule lines down it where the frames would have been, so that the dowels of the planking will appear correctly placed in the finished model. When the transom has been fully planked and the glue has had time to dry, trim down the ends of the planks so that they are flush with the surface of the side planking.

The next items to go on will be the transom end-timbers which, as will be seen from *Sketch No.* 35, run up the corners of the transom and cover the ends of the planks just laid, together with their joints with the side planking. When fixing the wale we stopped it short of the actual stern, and the breadth of the end-timber has to be such as to fill this space from the end of the wale to the face of the transom planking. Its thwartship breadth has to be the same as the width of the wale in plan, and from this it tapers until at the top the thwartship thickness is equal to the amount the rail projects from the planking. All this will be clear from the last named sketch. The quarter-badges and scroll boards we will leave until later.

We now have the choice of fitting either the anchor-deck or the quarterdeck, and I am all in favour of the latter, for if the former is installed the bowsprit will have to go in place too, and the longer we can keep the hull free of fixed projections the better. The quarterdeck beams will be made just as were those of the main, and although most of them extend only one-third out from the side, they should all be made full length in the first instance. The rise-of-beam template used for the maindeck beams will of course also apply here, as will the small jig used for fixing the depth of the ends, except that in the present case it will fix the top of the beams so that they are exactly the thickness of the deck planking below the top of the bulwarks instead of the wale. The deck planks must finish flush with the top edge of the upper strake of the bulwarks, so that when the bulwark capping rail goes on it will rest on both and act as a covering-board. When all the beams have been cut out they should be varnished and laid aside to dry, and while that is taking place we can fit one or two small details inside the bulwarks.

The fore-sheet comes in through a sheave fitted in a slot in a rail on the inside of the bulwarks just abaft the midship cavil. These rails should be glued in place port and starboard, and fixed with one or two dowels through the planking. On this scale I did not fit a sheave in this rail, but merely drilled two holes representing the outside diameter of the "sheave", and then filed a shallow surface-slot between them, both inside and out. The oval mooring ports can now be drilled, using a small drill and opening out the hole to the required shape with a fine round file. I lined these holes with a very narrow strip sawn off the end of a bit of tube and squeezed to the required oval. These were made first and the holes filed up to fit them. In view of the fact that the bulwarks are only 1/32 in. thick, a doubler has to be glued on the inside before cutting these holes and fitting the pipes. I made the holes so that the tube liners were a tight push fit, but I also added just a smear of adhesive when pushing them home. This now represents all the fittings inside the bulwarks except the pin-rails, and these cannot be fitted until the capping-rail is on, so the bulwarks can now be given two or three coats of French polish if that is the final treatment or, painted if not, and when doing this do not forget to carry it right round the ship including that portion inside the quarterdeck and stern-frame.

When the inside of the bulwarks is dry, we can fit the beams for the after deck. Take up the first beam, which as you will have discovered in making it, falls between the tops of frame No. 18½ and not across the face of them. Cut the mortices for the carlings and then put this beam in position and hold it with clamps. Then do the same for the beam immediately abaft the after house, although as this falls across the face of its frame, it can be wedged in position. Next take up two lengths of the material which is to be used for the carlings and mark and cut them to fit into the beam mortices. These carlings are made from much wider stuff than was used for the maindeck, as their inner faces have to be cut to the curve of the after house. When the carlings have been fitted, take up the beams which have to form the half-beams on either side, and mark and cut them as was done for the maindeck. Also mark the carlings for the positions of the mortices for these beams. Now make a template of the plan of the after house, and placing the after end against the after beam so far fitted, run a pencil round the sides which will mark the curvature to be given to the inner faces of the carlings.

Lay aside the template which will be of service again when we come to building the house, then remove the carlings, cut the mortices in their outboard faces and the required curvature in the inboard ones, after which assemble the whole unit and fix in position as was done with the beams round the main hatch. The ends of the beams can either be fixed by dowelling into the frames, or by the use of filling-chocks, although the first beam, which is still a complete unit right across by the way, will have to be skew-dowelled into the frame in any case.

Now proceed to build the framework shown in *Sketch No.* 62, cut the two posts marked "A" from 1/8 in. x 1/8 in. and to one end glue and dowel a small block "B" for fixing to the deck. Put these posts in position and glue in the rails "C" along the deck and after dowelling where possible, leave to dry, after which the section of the beam marked "D" can be sawn out with a fine jeweller's saw, although personally I would leave this beam intact until actually fitting the house—which will be pre-fabricated—in position.

When the beam construction forming the opening for the after house is fitted, carry on with the remaining beam aft, and if you have used a proper stern frame instead of the fashion-piece, run a curved beam round the inside of this, or if you like, put in filling-chocks round the top. Either will do, the main thing being to provide a sound landing for the after ends of the deck planks.

The break of the quarterdeck should next be covered, and the best way to do this is to use a solid panel. Cut a template which will fit closely along the deck and into the bulwarks, then run a pencil along the top of the beam for the curvature of the quarterdeck. From this template cut a piece of 1/32 in. sycamore, then round the outer edges glue and dowel a margin of mahogany or walnut veneer, so making a complete panel as shown in the small drawing on *Sketch No.* 62. French polish this and when finished glue and dowel it to the face of the quarterdeck framing, then treat the other side of the deck in the same way.

To some readers the dowelling of small veneer panels may perhaps seem rather unnecessary, feeling that a glued joint would be sufficient. Well perhaps they may be right, but I have always made it a rule never to leave *anything* to an adhesive fixing if it is at all possible to pin or dowel it as well, and by using the latter there are very few things which cannot be dowelled, for one can get bamboo into material where even the finest pin would be quite impossible. I think that in the long run the policy of dowelling everything pays dividends, and as an example of this I would site the model Norwegian barque which appears in the group in photograph *Fig.* 3. This model was built in 1920, 38 years ago, and is completely rigged down to buntlines and clewlines, with linen sails furled along the yards. It has all deck fittings, including a full working steering gear inside the wheelbox on the quarterdeck, while all running rigging is taken down to the deck and belayed on pins. Yet this model has never seen the inside of a case; for the whole of those 38 years it has stood on a shelf in the office, exposed to all the temperature and atmospheric changes of our climate, to say nothing of the none-too-kind administrations of various office cleaners, while the periodical accumulation of dust can well be imagined.

In my previous office I had a convenient flat roof outside one of the windows, and when the dust coating got too bad the model was put out on this for five or six hours of a pouring wet day—I aways picked a good one! Just before the office closed it was brought in again and left over the sink to drain, being returned to its shelf next morning as good as new. The office occupied since the war has no such convenient roof, so the cleansing treatment has become more drastic, for when the dust gets too thick the model is taken into the print room and placed in one of the large print washing baths, there it is hosed down with a 1" hose and a fair pressure of water until clean, after which it is left to dry. This last method results in a lot of water finding its way below through the open hatches, etc., and she usually finishes full right up to the deckhead, for it takes a lot of hosing to get rid of the thick dust clinging to the sails and the web of rigging, much of which is about three times its true size by the time she is due for her wash. The decks too get full of dirt almost up to the level of the pin-rails, and for a time the water runs from the scuppers like washing decks after a coal cargo. However filling up inside merely gives this a wash too, and pumping-ship is quite a simple matter. Right forward in the bows she has two removable timberheads, and when these are taken out and the vessel held bow down, two powerful jets of water shoot out of the holes so provided, as well as a good cascade along the deck from the hatch as soon as she is up-ended. When she has had time to drain, she is returned to her shelf to start another accumulation.

The only result of this rather harsh treatment has been that she now needs a new ensign, but neither hull, rigging nor fittings have suffered in the least, and nothing has ever come adrift, in fact she gets more likeable ac time goes on, gaining the real "atmosphere" of her type all the time. She never did have any polish, for that is one thing I do not like in a model, but as the result of her rough treatment she has become "weathered" and looks, at least to me, just right for a small sailing merchantman.

I appreciate that a glass case model would not be expected to stand this treatment, but I do say that such a model would probably have double the life as the result of being dowelled throughout. One often sees fine old models, including those which have been well cared for, with some small items adrift here and there. In really good models it is probable that all major items have been pinned or dowelled, but that the builder has thought it sufficient to glue the small features such as door panels or scrolls. Personally I think such features need dowels every bit as much as the larger items, since the glue has to be applied very frugally if it is not to mark adjacent features, also it is often impossible to apply to such small items the pressure so necessary for a good glued joint. In my models I work on the principle that *everything*, down to the most minute particle of veneer, must be dowelled as well as glued, using in some places dowels as fine as a No. 80 drill, which is quite possible from bamboo. Later on I will be referring to some models made while on service during the war. These had to be dependent on adhesive, and in several places they are showing signs of coming adrift, so throughout this book I will continue to suggest that all items be "glued and dowelled", leaving the reader to please himself as to whether he follows that advice or not.

Now back to planking. The quarterdeck is largely made up of the narrow alleyways on either side of the house, so the planking runs parallel to the ship's side, which simplifies matters since there will be no need to joggle the ends into a margin-plank. Abaft the house the planks meet in a king-plank on the centreline, but this is so short that only very few planks will have to be joggled. Before starting to lay the deck, the single thwartship planks should be laid along the top of the beam at the break. This plank is so placed that it slightly overhangs the edge and so forms a "nosing" over the head of the panelled bulkhead as shown in the section on *Sketch No.* 62. Glue and dowel this nosing-plank along the top of the beam on either side of the house—or rather, at this stage, the opening for the house—so that its inner edge runs along the centre of the beam, leaving the other half available to form a landing for the planks of the deck.

The curvature of the ship's side is relatively small along the quarters, so there will be no need to cut the planks to this, instead give them a prebending in some form of jig, such as that shown in *Sketch No.* 48, although of course with much less curve and with the planks bent on edge. After they are bent cut them into the usual lengths, i.e. 2½ in. to 3 in., and start at the fore end, fitting the plank end to the angle of the nosing-plank, then laying it with its outboard edge close against the inside of the top strake of the bulwarks. Mark the other end to land on a suitable beam, then glue and dowel in position. Continue in the same way right along to the stern, cutting it off so that it will fit just inside the transom planking, the joint being later covered by the capping-rail when that is put on. It is an advantage to treat this deck as we did the hull planking, and work each strake from either end, since it is often easier to meet in a square joint than finish with the angular joint at the transom, but that is a matter of opinion.

When you have one complete plank running from break to transom, proceed to lay the same plank on the other side of the deck, for it is most important that the two sides should be identical, not only because you must meet the house with the same width of plank on either side, but also to ensure that the joggles in the king-plank will be matched. Continue planking, first one side and then the other until the two belts are about to meet at the stern. Now cut a piece of material double the width of the planking used, and long enough to reach from the after side of the opening for the house to the stern. Lay this down on the centreline of the ship, but merely hold it to the beams with a couple of pins. As soon as the deck planking starts to over-ride this king-plank, mark it and joggle the end of the plank. Run a sharp pencil round the joggle and then cut the king-plank to receive it. Carry on in this way until the whole after deck is planked, then lift the king-plank, mark and cut out the top of the rudder-trunk, then glue and dowel the king-plank in position and your deck should appear as in *Sketch No.* 63. The deck can now be cleaned up and polished.

Some builders may prefer to make the house first and build the deck round it, but I think that a mistake, for while that would allow the deck car-lings to be fitted to the side of the house and the half beams worked into them, by leaving the house until later you have much greater freedom to work, With a completely clear deck for the final rubbing down and polish-ing. There is also the fact that the house, which will have been pre-fabri-cated, can be kept out of the model until a later date, and so be safe from scratching or other damage while laying the deck and doing other work about the model. The house will be made so that it will drop into place as a complete Unit, yet show no join with the deck or carlings.

In *Leon* the quarterdeck planking follows the ship's side, but in ships with an open quarterdeck or full poop the planks will most probably be laid parallel to the centreline and joggled into a margin plank as the side nar-rows in at the stern, so perhaps I had better say something about laying a deck of this kind. The actual arrangement of the deck edge on poops and fo'castles of wooden ships varied to some extent, but one thing is cer-tain, the common model practice of allowing the actual deck to overhang the sides was not one of them; even modern steel ships, in which we have no interest at the moment, usually had the plating carried up an inch or so above the deck level so that an angle could be run round inside to make a tight joint between deck and side, yet most model builders seem to be quite content—and I was one of them for many years—to simply place the poop deck on top of the sides and let it overhang. In wooden ships the most usual arrangement was to construct the poop and fo'castle on the same lines as the maindeck, complete with covering-board and waterway, the only real differences being that of size and the fact that open rails, either wood or iron, took the place of the bulwarks. *Sketch No.* 64A. In some the waterway was more shallow as in "*B*". Composite ships were dif-ferent of course, because as a rule they had an iron sheer-strake under the planking of the topsides, as well as a partly iron deck below the wood-en one, so that their deck edges, as far as poop and fo'castle were con-cerned, often followed ironship practice.

To go back to *Sketch No.* 64. The covering-board runs on top of the timberheads (frames) and waterway, which latter runs inside the tops of the frames. Then inside the waterway is another plank, the margin-plank, which also follows the shape of the ship's side but unlike the waterway, is of the same thickness as the deck planks, and it is into this margin that the latter are joggled. The rule is that if the deck plank meets the margin plank at such an angle that the length of the bevel "Y" is less than the breadth of the plank "X", *Sketch No.* 65A, the plank need not be joggled,

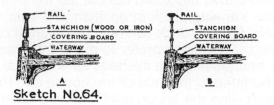

Sketch No.64.

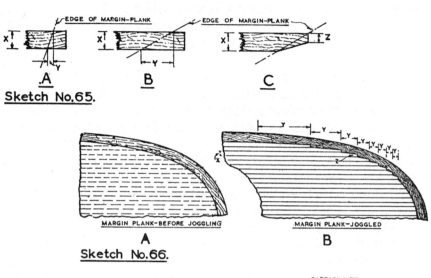

Sketch No.65.

MARGIN PLANK—BEFORE JOGGLING

A

MARGIN PLANK—JOGGLED

B

Sketch No.66.

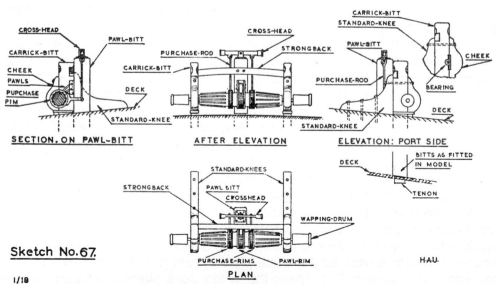

SECTION, ON PAWL-BITT

AFTER ELEVATION

ELEVATION: PORT SIDE

Sketch No.67.

PLAN

H·A·U·

but if "Y" exceeds "X" (65B), then the end must be joggled. The cutting of the joggle is simple, the square toe "Z" being made half the width of the plank and the margin-plank cut accordingly. *Sketch No.* 66 shows part of a deck before and after cutting the joggles in the margin plank.

The scuppers of the maindeck may or may not be fitted on a small scale model, for they would be only about 3/64 in. diameter on *Leon*, but if you wish to drill them they will run down through the covering board and out on top of the wale. In full-size practice they were lined with a length of lead pipe which was then flanged out at each end.

The next job will be to make the bowsprit, a full-size drawing of which is included on the Spar Detail Sheet of the set of plans for building this model, it is also illustrated in Vol. II. When I built my model I not only made the bowsprit at this stage, but also fixed it, however I think that if I were doing the job again I would not actually fix it, but merely leave it in position while making the small forward deck, then take it out again until I was ready to rig the ship. This would mean the final fixing would have to be outside the deck instead of below it but there really is no objection to a dowel down into the stemhead outboard, instead of inboard as in my case, this dowel can be placed below the jibboom heel-chock where it will be completely hidden. Doing this will also mean that all one needs now will be the bare spar, whereas if it is to be fixed at once, then all the fittings will have to go on it.

The heel of the bowsprit has a tenon which fits into a mortice in a stout timber bolted to two upright posts which come up through the deck just forward of the hawse-pipes. In full-size practice these posts go down through the deck and step on either side of the forward deadwood, but in the model I made a small tenon on the bottom of each and these registered in holes in the deck, into which they were glued after the whole assembly had been made. Across the faces of these two posts a piece of 3/8 in. x 1/8 in. sycamore was glued and dowelled, with the mortice for the bowsprit tenon in the centre of it. This tenon should be square, but I made it round and drilled the mortice accordingly. The only thing to watch in this job is that the hole forming the mortice is drilled at the correct angle. The tops of the two posts should just register with the underside of the anchor-deck when that is in position, so that a dowel can be driven down through the deck into each post, which makes a good strong job.

Put the bowsprit in place and fix it to the stemhead with a pin driven down through the hole which will ultimately be used for the dowel, then mark out and cut the beams for the anchor-deck, but do not fit them. Now you will have to decide just how you intend to set up the forestay, whether you are going to take the ends of the stay down to the eye-bolts in the knight heads as in the ship and shown on the plans and *Sketch No.* 61A or whether you follow an arrangement found in many ships where this stay is set up well inboard, in which the actual fixing was brought above the light deck by means of metal bar as in *No.* 61*B,* or some other form of fixing which will bring the eyes of the rigging out to deck level. If you follow the original ship then you will have to fix the ends of the stay before you make the anchordeck. The forestay is double, that is to say it goes from the eye-bolt in one knighthead, up and round the mast, then down again to the eye-bolt on the other knighthead. In full-size practice these ends of the stay would be passed down through the holes in the deck, taken round the thimble at the eyebolt, then back up through the hole again, where they would be set up taut by means of tackles on their own standing-parts. A man below the light deck would put on a seizing close to the thimble, while two more seizings were put on above deck and all would be set up. In the model the best way of doing this is to put all three seizings on one side, then pass the stay up through one hole in the deck—before the latter is fixed of course, then allow enough material to go up round the mast and down again, passing the end down through the other hole in the deck; through the eye in the knighthead, back through the hole in the deck and cut off, leaving plenty of spare.

In setting up the stay after the masts are in, it would be put over the masthead, then the end which had no seizings would be worked through the eye until the stay was taut, after which the two seizings above the deck would be put on and the surplus cut off. In this way the stay would be rigged as in the actual ship except that the seizing below the deck on one side would be missing. The only real disadvantage of this arrangement is that the length of double stay has to be kicking about the ship all the time the small deck forward is being fitted, and throughout the making and fixing of all the deck fittings. Of course this method of setting up the stay will not apply to all models, in fact to relatively few, for in most cases the forestay was taken out to the bowsprit just clear of the stem.

This light deck forward is one which can be laid on top of a bit of 1/32 in. sycamore or plywood, the bend will be one way only, that of the beams, for in that short length the sheer is not noticeable. I cut out a cardboard template and fitted it round the heel of the bowsprit and marked it for the position of the beams, then from this I cut a piece of 1/32 in. sycamore. Remember that the top of the finished deck must be flush with the top strake of the bulwarks, so that the rail will sit on both. Before finally fitting this deck however it will be as well to consider the windlass, since the standard-knees, or carrick-knees, of this run back under the overhanging deck, and unless put in first, they will be difficult to fix. There is a full-size drawing of the windlass in the plans, while it is also shown in S*ketch No.* 67. I made the windlass from some scraps of cedar, which worked up very well. The main side timbers or carrick-bitts should go right down through the deck and be stepped in the heavy timbers of the ceiling, after being

Fig. 17.
Author's model ready for rigging.

BRIGANTINE *LEON*

Fig. 18.
Quarterdeck of **Professor Favez's** model.

Fig.19. Fore deck of model by Mr. J. Bracamontes of Coyoacan.

Fig. 20.
Model Dutch fishing vessel under construction.
by Mr. H. M. Kolstee of New York.

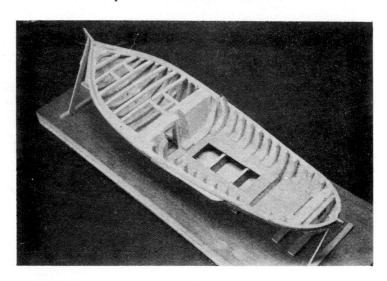

bolted to deckbeams and special carlings on the way, but in the model I cheated over this. As I have already said I did not fit any ceiling so there was nothing to step them in anyway. Instead of taking them right through the deck, I merely formed a long tenon on the bottom of each and cut a corresponding mortice in the deck to take it. The carrick-bitts were put in place but not glued, while templates were made for the carrick-knees. These were then glued and dowelled to the bitts. next the strongback was cut out and glued and dowelled into the slots provided in the carrick-bitts, and finally the cheeks cut and dowelled in place. My lathe was not available when this model was built, so I roughly carved the barrel, then, having left an end on to be gripped in the chuck, I "turned" it where necessary in an ordinary breast drill by means of warding files while someone turned the handle. The two ratchet wheels, or purchase-rims, and the central pawl-rim were "turned" and the teeth filed or scribed on the latter. The warping-drums then turned and short lengths of wire were inserted in them and pushed through holes in the cheeks and into the ends of the barrel. The cross-head, dummy pawls and operating gear, *Sketch No. 68*, were made later. When the assembly was complete, the carrick-bitts were glued into the mortices in the deck, the knees glued and dowelled to the deck, and finally the strongback dowelled to the pawl-bitt. As I have already said I did not complete the job at this stage as I thought that the crosshead might get damaged while fitting the anchor-deck and cat-heads, but I may as well finish the windlass on paper and the reader can please himself whether he does the rest of the work later. The cross-head and supporting bracket were made as two pieces, both filed up from heavy copper wire which had first been hammered square. They were silver soldered together and fixed to the pawl-bitt by a spike left on the bottom for that purpose. The dummy link motion was made of brass wire. The general effect was what I wanted, but it does not work! The metal straps, which in the full-size windlass bind the cheeks to the carrick-bitts, were made as I made all such metal work, from thin copper wire hammered out flat and then cleaned up with a fine file.

With the main body of the windlass in position the deck beams can now be fitted, the 1/32 in. deck glued and dowelled in place and then planked in veneer. Incidentally for making planks of this material I use the tool shown in *Sketch No. 69*, which consists of two razor blades held between plates and separated by a packer representing the width of plank required. These packers may either be blocks of hardwood of different thicknesses according to the width of plank required, or better still, a few metal plates of different thicknesses, various combinations of which would provide a wide range of plank widths. The only point to watch with this tool is that the projection of the blades beyond the side plates and packer is kept as small as possible, only just sufficient to go through the material to

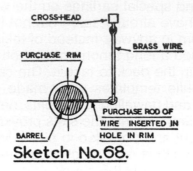

CROSS-HEAD

BRASS WIRE

PURCHASE RIM

PURCHASE ROD OF
WIRE INSERTED IN
HOLE IN RIM

BARREL

Sketch No.68.

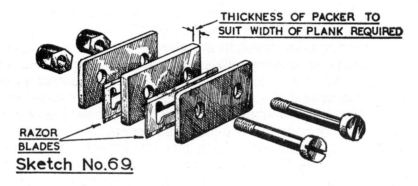

THICKNESS OF PACKER TO
SUIT WIDTH OF PLANK REQUIRED

RAZOR
BLADES

Sketch No.69.

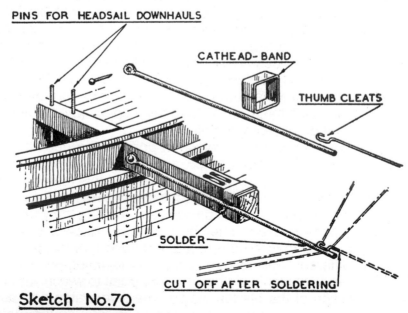

PINS FOR HEADSAIL DOWNHAULS

CATHEAD–BAND

THUMB CLEATS

SOLDER

CUT OFF AFTER SOLDERING

Sketch No.70.

be cut. Razor blades are very flexible, and if allowed to project more than absolutely necessary, a little extra pressure will tend to make them spread and the width of the plank vary.

In the ship the catheads support the after end of the light anchor deck by having a rail bolted along their lower inside edges to receive the ends of the deck planks, but in the model I carried the deck right out to the after faces of the catheads, which were in fact glued and dowelled down to it. The catheads were made from 1/8 in. square hardwood, tapered inboard as shown in the plans. The two sheaves in the outer end of each were dummy, small holes being drilled through representing the top and bottom of each sheave, and then the wood scored between them to represent the sheavehole. The hole for the inboard bolt of the whisker-booms, *Sketch No. 70*, was drilled, but none of the metal work made at this stage because the projecting wire would have caught in everything which came near it.

The bulwark capping-rail can now be fitted, and for this I used some 1/16 in. mahogany. Start at the bow and make the first section, which extends from the bowsprit to cathead. Do not try to bend material for this rail, but cut out each section from strips wide enough to allow for this, and I think it pays to make a cardboard template for each piece, getting this a good fit so that you will know that when once cut out, the actual rail will go in place without any spring. This forward section will be glued and dowelled to the deck, as will be the portion which goes round the quarterdeck, but midships it will be glued to the top of the bulwark planking, and glued and dowelled to the top of every stanchion. Run this rail right out to the stern on either side, then mitre the after ends and fit a similar rail across the top of the transom, closing the joint between the deck and the transom planking. The width of this rail round the ship should be as shown on the plans, but first check the moulded thickness of your bulwark stanchions and if necessary make the breadth of your rail accordingly, it should project about 1/64 in. over both stanchions and external bulwark planking. Round the quarter deck it must not be less than 3/32 in. wide to receive the wash-strake or bottom rail of the timber guard-rail.

The pin-rails inside the bulwarks will be the next items to go in and these should be made from say 1/8 in. x 1/16 in. mahogany. The finished width is 3/32 in. but the 1/8 in. material will allow for fitting to the slight curvature of the hull, and above all, for fitting to get good contact with the inside of the main-rail. This latter is most important since the only support for the pinrails is their contact at this point. Most of the running-rigging sets up on these rails and it is possible to get a fair amount of pull on them, so they must be firmly fixed. You would be in a nice mess if one of these rails came away when you were belaying the gear, for by that time all the standing-rigging would be in place, and getting at the pin-rail would be no

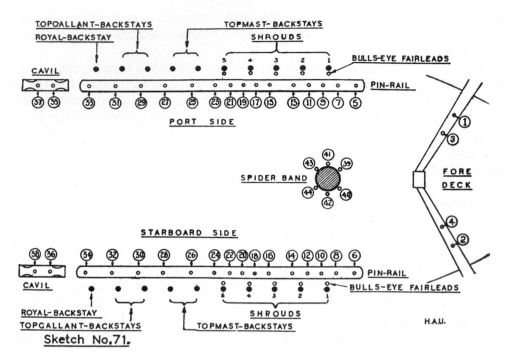

Sketch No. 71.

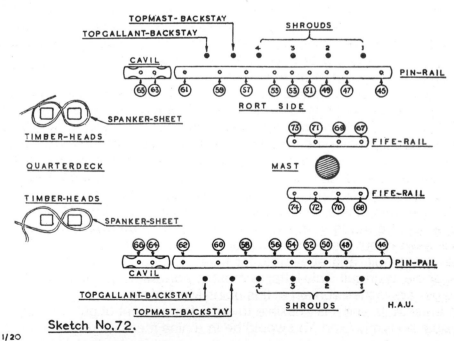

Sketch No. 72.

1/20

easy job.

I made and fitted these rails after the mainrail, or capping-rail was in place, but I think if I were doing the job again I would fit them to the latter before it went into place, in which case I would have glued both mainrail and pin-rail down on a piece of good tough brown paper, then when dry cleaned them up and cut them out, leaving the paper undisturbed on the under side. I would then have varnished over this before fitting, and finally dowelled right through both rails, just as you will have to do when fitting them separately. If you do fit them after the mainrail is in position, still glue the pin-rail down on to a bit of stiff brown paper, then when you cut it out leave about 1/32 in. of paper overhanging on the edge which goes to the mainrail, so that when in position this paper will be stuck to the underside of the mainrail, and so cover and stiffen the whole joint, after which the rails should be drilled right through and either dowels or pins driven through. A pair of small hardwood angle brackets glued to the bulwarks and the underside of the pin-rail will also give additional strength to this important item, or a post carried down to the deck at either end would serve the same purpose

For the number and position of belaying pin holes in relation to the shrouds see *Sketches No. 71 and 72*, which show the fore and main masts respectively. The belaying-pin numbers refer to the belaying table which will be given with the running-rigging in Vol. II.

The hull is now complete but for the wash-strake round the edge of the anchor-deck, and the wash-strake and rails of the quarterdeck, but I think we will include these with the deck fittings, since the latter might be open to damage if put on too early.

I have several times made the point that *Leon's* deck construction was not common to many vessels, and certainly not to the larger class of ship. The more normal construction for larger vessels, and most smaller ones too, is that shown in the midship section *Sketch No. 43* and the perspective sections *Sketch No. 73*. From these drawings it will be seen that the beams were carried on the beam-shelf as already described, but the frames extended well above the tops of the beams, so that a heavy timber, the waterway, ran all round the ship inside the timbers (frames) and on top of the beams. This timber was often much heavier than the shelf and provided much of the strength of the vessel at this level. Its upper surface was flush with the tops of the timbers, between which filling-chocks occupied the space from waterway to inside of the hull planking, and to the depth of the waterway, the whole being sealed on top by the covering-board, so that a solid belt of timber extended round the hull. The effect of this was that covering-board and waterway combined formed a step some 12 in. or 18 in. above the deck inside the bulwarks.

The waterways varied slightly in shape, some being concave and oth-

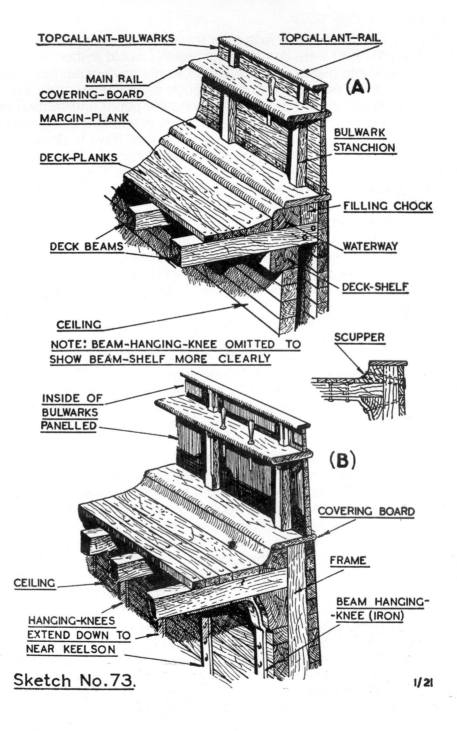

TOPGALLANT–BULWARKS   TOPGALLANT–RAIL

MAIN RAIL
COVERING–BOARD

MARGIN–PLANK

DECK–PLANKS

(A)

BULWARK
STANCHION

FILLING CHOCK

DECK BEAMS

WATERWAY

DECK-SHELF

CEILING

NOTE: BEAM-HANGING-KNEE OMITTED TO
SHOW BEAM-SHELF MORE CLEARLY

SCUPPER

INSIDE OF
BULWARKS
PANELLED

(B)

COVERING BOARD

CEILING

FRAME

HANGING-KNEES
EXTEND DOWN TO
NEAR KEELSON

BEAM HANGING-
-KNEE (IRON)

Sketch No. 73.

1/21

ers convex on their inboard faces, while other ships had an inner water-way with a slope on top which tended to reduce the apparent height of the step. The general effect of this construction was that while the covering board when seen from outboard clearly indicated the sheer-strake and top of the hull, it did not show the level of the deck, which might in a few small vessels such as *Leon* be immediately below it, but would more common-ly be anything from one to two feet below. This is a point often overlooked in models, where the old idea that the level of the deck must be seen from outside the hull dies hard. The sheer line as seen from the outside of the hull may have no relation whatever to the run of the deck although in British wooden ships it usually did, but not at the same level. However quite a number of ships did have their decks at a different fore and aft rise to the bulwarks, which might be say 4 ft. 6 ins. midships and 6 ft. 0 ins. at the break of the fo'castle. In the big American schooners, the sheer often swept up from the rail being flush with the deck midships, to five or six feet above it forward, an open fly-rail being run along the top of the rail as pro-tection midships; although forward, this rail would be overhead. This ques-tion of deck level is one which the model builder must examine with care before starting work, for on it will depend the arrangement of all deck beams, also how far beyond the level of the deck he has to carry the frames.

In most ships the bulwark stanchions will be separate spars, passing through holes on the covering-board and filling-chocks, to extend some six feet down the face of a frame, to which it will be bolted. The tops of these stanchions may either be at the level of the mainrail, in which case the to'gallant stanchions will be stepped in mortices in the latter, or the main bulwark stanchion may be "shouldered" at the mainrail, above which it will continue and so form the stanchion of the to'gallant bulwarks. The planking of the bulwarks will be relatively thin as in the *Leon* model, but generally with two strakes of slightly thicker material, one immediately below the mainrail and the other on top of the covering-board, giving the side a slightly "stepped" effect top and bottom. This brings out another point often overlooked in models, and that is that in wooden ships the bul-warks are almost invariably slightly set back from the main hull, and that to make a model of a wooden ship flush-sided will, in 99 cases out of 100, be completely wrong, yet how often one sees such models.

In the average merchant ship the inside of the bulwarks will be quite plain as in *Sketch No. 73A*, but the passenger ships and clippers were generally panelled as in *Sketch No. 73B*, while the big East Indiaman, which was built on naval lines, had the inside of the bulwarks planked and panelled so that the stanchions were hidden. The mainrail, which was of course also the pin-rail, will be carried full width for the whole length of the deck.

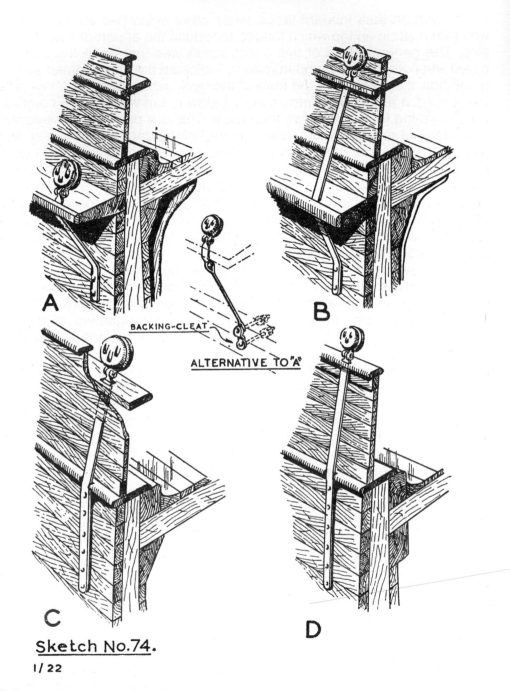

BACKING-CLEAT

ALTERNATIVE TO "A"

A

B

C

D

Sketch No. 74.

1/22

The method of setting up the standing rigging is another point on which the model builder must know his particular ship, but the most common arrangement for the real "old-stagers" was the broad channel on the level of the deck beams, *Sketch No. 74A*. A modification of this was the double channel, in which the chain-plates, the iron straps to which the dead-eyes were attached, extended through to the upper channel so bringing the lower dead-eye to rail level, *Sketch No. 74B*. Later ships dispensed with channels altogether and bolted the chain-plates directly on to the sitle of the hull, with their upper ends slotted through the bulwarks to bring the dead-eyes out on top of the mainrail, *Sketch No. 74C*, while *Leon* and other small vessels which had only one rail, carried the chain-plates along the bulwarks and only slotted this last rail, bringing the dead-eye out to its centreline *Sketch No. 74D*. Another very common feature was the use of a backingcleat as shown in the small inset sketch. These cleats were used in *Leon*.

CHAPTER V

DECK ERECTIONS, FITTINGS AND FINISH.

WE will finish the outside of the hull before making any of the deck fittings or furnishings, and the best place to start will be the bill-boards. These serve two main purposes, to protect the hull from damage by the flukes of the anchor when it is being got aboard, and also make a smooth surface over which it may slide. The hull as it is at present has a number of projections; the wale, rail, and the fact that the thinner bulwark planking sits back from the face of the hull proper. These projections would soon be torn to shreds by the anchors if left as they are, and to prevent this, heavy timber, which could be replaced when badly worn, was fitted on the ship's side to protect them. It filled the bulwarks and covered the wale, below which it was washed away into the planking of the hull. Bill-boards were, in later days, usually faced with iron plates.

In the model these bill-boards can either be made from the solid, all in one piece, and carefully fitted over the wale and into the bulwarks; or they may be put on in two sections, one above and one below the wale. Whichever method is used they must he a good fit on the face of the hull, to which they are glued and dowelled. Their shape and size can be taken from the plans, and their position is such that when the shackle of the anchor is at the end of the cathead, the crown and flukes of the anchor will make contact with the bill-boards.

We now come to the scrollwork on the bow, quarter-badges and transom, which will prove a most interesting job, even to those who may have no gift for carving. I think the scroll-work on my own model will pass muster, in spite of the fact that it was produced in a must unorthodox manner. I have no small wood carving tools, so I made my scrolls by half cutting, half scraping until I reached the required depth. All scrolls were made in the same way, the only difference being that those at the bow had to be given both considerable curvature and a half-twist, and for this it is best to make a cardboard template before cutting out the wood, in fact templates for all of them will save quite a lot of trouble later on.

Take a piece of 1/16 in. sycamore, box, or any other very close grain wood, cut it out from your template, and then draw on it the scrolls to be cut, or if you are not very good at this kind of thing, make a tracing of the scrolls as shown on the plans, then turn this face down on your piece of wood. Now go over the back of the lines very carefully and you will have transferred your tracing to the surface of the wood, but more than that, you will also have made a new tracing for the scroll on the other side of the ship, which will of course be the opposite hand, for if you now place your tracing on another piece of wood, the original face up this time, and again go over the lines, you will have the opposite scroll on the wood. One point here, use a fairly hard pencil and see that it is *sharp*. When you have transferred your scrolls to the wood—sycamore being almost pure white is ideal for this job—go over the lines with pencil just to strengthen them, for they will get quite a lot of rubbing while being "carved".

I then made my carving tools by breaking a steel knitting needle into several pieces and grinding them down to form small cutting tools, some with square ends and others at an angle. These I inserted in strong pen holders and I was ready to start. Using one of the tools as a simple cutter I carefully cut all round the edge of the scroll, afterwards half-cutting half-scraping, I removed the wood from round about and between the various turns of the scroll, holding it up to the light from time to time to judge the depth to which I had cut it. I continued in this way until the base between the scrolls was so thin that one could see daylight through it. This may sound very difficult but it is not, it requires patience particularly if working with home-made tools such as mine, but providing care is taken with the cutting of the outline in the first instance, the removal of the wood between the scrolls is quite simple, just a matter of cutting and scraping away until the required depth is reached. Do not attempt to smooth off the tool marks from the recessed part of the work, even in full-size work such portions of a carving would show these marks. In any case these recessed portions should be made so thin that they merely form a kind of backing film for the scrolls themselves. When finished, the scroll should be lightly rubbed over with very fine sandpaper, after which it is glued and dowelled in position on the hull. The ultimate finish will depend upon the treatment the hull as a whole is to receive, if it is to be painted, then the actual scrolls will perhaps be gilt against a painted ground, but if the finish is to be "natural" as with my own model, a good effect will be obtained by giving the recessed base say two coats of stain, just to make it a little darker than the face of the scroll, or of course vice versa.

Your first attempt may turn out very poor; very well, do not use it but try again, a few scraps of sycamore are not very important, and time spent experimenting is never time wasted. Of course it is no use trying to make these scrolls from an open-grain wood, that *would* be a waste of time, but with something like box or sycamore a little practice will produce reasonable results.

The more general deck fittings really need very little description, for their details are given in the plans, and the construction of such fittings differs little for plank-built or solid hull. The metal fairleads fore and aft I filed up from bits of brass, while the small warping capstan on the anchordeck was "turned" from hardwood. The pumps and navel-pipes were built of bits of brass tube and brass sheet, silver soldered. The anchors are also fabricated, and their dimensions and construction will be clear from *Sketch No.* 75, the material being heavy gauge sheet brass. At the time of the photograph included in this book, *Leon* carried an old wood-stocked anchor to port, but I doubt whether this really represented the type she carried in her prime. I will have a little more to say about this photograph in Vol. II., but when it was taken she was near the end of her days and signs of poverty were to be seen all over her. The hull was almost entirely devoid of paint, and much of her gear had obviously come from other vessels, so I see no reason why the wood-stocked anchor may not be included in the latter. I suggest giving the model the type shown in the drawings, but should the reader favour a wood-stocked one, well the photograph is there to prove that she did at one period carry such an anchor.

I have not yet reached the stage of fitting the chain cable in the *Leon* model, but this will have to be done before the job can be regarded as complete. Small size stud-link cable is not very easy to come by these days, but as I usually make my own this is not a very serious matter. The making of small chain, either plain or stud-link is not really difficult, and I will be describing my methods in Volume II.

The construction of the houses, companions and skylights in my model was on the principle of an internal shell, on which the rails and stiles of the panels were superimposed. *Sketch No.* 76 illustrates the fo'-castle companion. The shell is made of 1/16 in sycamore, with the top shaped to the curve required and the "skirt" a tight push-fit in the hole in the deck. Glue and dowel the corners, and when dry put the shell in position in the hole in the deck and after checking for height, run a sharp pencil round it at deck level. The skirt by the way should project into the hull to the depth of the beams. One other point I seem to have failed to mention, after cutting out the shell, rule the inside faces in pencil to represent planks, and then stain them before glueing together, for it is just possible to see the inside of this companion if it is left open. Having marked the line of the deck all round the shell, remove it and proceed to glue and dowel veneer on the outside to form the rails and stiles round the panels. The top is also made of veneer, glued and dowelled to the shell. If the companion is to be shown open, then the after side of the shell will stop short of the top to allow the drop panel to hang down. The hinges and other metal fittings I made in my usual manner, from copper wire of the required size, hammered flat and dressed with a fine file. These hinges were all dummy in my model, the panel being dowelled in the open position and so fixed

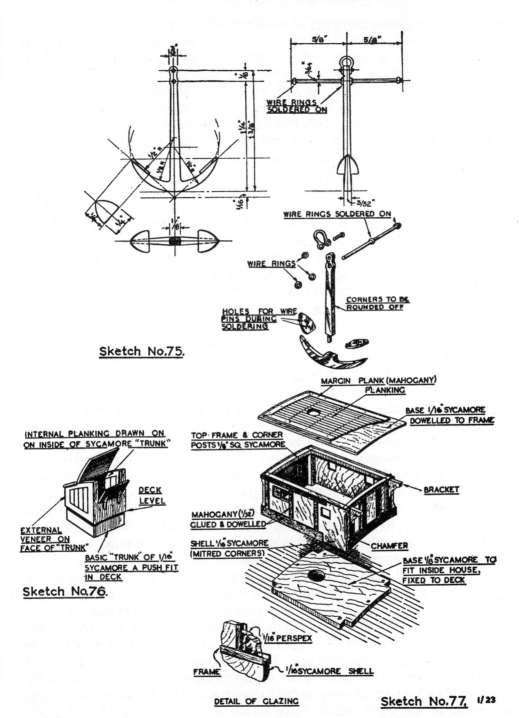

WIRE RINGS SOLDERED ON

WIRE RINGS SOLDERED ON

WIRE RINGS

HOLES FOR WIRE PINS DURING SOLDERING

CORNERS TO BE ROUNDED OFF

Sketch No.75.

MARGIN PLANK (MAHOGANY)
PLANKING

BASE 1/16" SYCAMORE DOWELLED TO FRAME

INTERNAL PLANKING DRAWN ON ON INSIDE OF SYCAMORE "TRUNK"

TOP FRAME & CORNER POSTS 1/8" SQ. SYCAMORE

DECK LEVEL

BRACKET

MAHOGANY (1/32") GLUED & DOWELLED

EXTERNAL VENEER ON FACE OF "TRUNK"

BASIC "TRUNK" OF 1/16" SYCAMORE A PUSH FIT IN DECK

SHELL 1/16" SYCAMORE (MITRED CORNERS)

CHAMFER

BASE 1/16" SYCAMORE TO FIT INSIDE HOUSE, FIXED TO DECK

Sketch No.76.

1/16" PERSPEX

FRAME

1/16" SYCAMORE SHELL

DETAIL OF GLAZING

Sketch No.77. 1/23

permanently, but from samples of workmanship sent me from time to time by correspondents, I know that many would have no difficulty in producing a scale working hinge for this job. I confess that very fine metal work is not a strong point with me, although strangely enough I enjoy making small metal mast fittings. Perhaps it is just "ironmongery" I do not like! When the panelwork is complete, try the companion in position, where the veneer skirting should completely hide the junction with the deck. If all is satisfactory the fitting can be removed again and either polished or varnished, and kept in a safe place while the rest of the work is taken in hand. When the time arrives to finally fit all the houses, etc., in position, the skirt of the companion will be coated with glue and pushed home into the hole in the deck.

The forward house can now be taken in hand, and here again the shell is of 1/16 in. sycamore. The finished corners of this house are chamfered, so it will be necessary to mitre the corners of the shell, *Sketch No. 77*. All openings for doors and lights are of course cut out before the shell is assembled, also remember to mark out the camber of both top and bottom of the end members, using the "rise-of-beam" template and finally fitting to the finished deck. The corners of the shell are strengthened by 1/8 in. square verticals glued and dowelled in position, while a frame of the same material is run round the top both to stiffen it and also form a landing for the roof or deck of the house. Remember to bevel the tops of these side rails to the camber, otherwise the base of the roof will not make good contact. The roof of this house overhangs at the after end and is supported by timber brackets at either side; these must be cut and glued and dowelled in position before the shell is assembled, otherwise there will be difficulty in driving the dowels. The external panels are formed of mahogany veneer, glued and dowelled in position, which makes a nice contrast with the light sycamore base. When the body of the house is complete, lay it on a sheet of 1/4 in. or 1/8 in. sycamore and run a pencil round the inside, then cut the sheet to this, making it a good push-fit inside the house. Bend or hollow out the underside of this sheet to fit the maindeck, to which it should be glued and screwed as shown in the sketch, not forgetting to leave a good clear hole for the mast to pass through. This hole will not be seen, so leave plenty of room round the mast to allow for final adjustment of rake, etc. When finished the house should sit tightly over this base.

The lights are glazed with 1/16 in. perspex, cut a neat fit for the holes in the shell, then glued on the edges and pushed home, a frame of veneer being fitted, slightly overlapping the perspex, both inside and out, although the inner one need not be made to scale width. The tops of the houses are of 1/16 in. sycamore, cut to overhang the sides 1/16 in., except of course at the ends which have to be extended over the brackets. Carefully set out the position of the mast hole, and drill this 1/8 in. or 5/32 in. larger than the actual diameter of the mast at that level, also rule across the top the positions which the beams would occupy in the full-size house. This sheet should now be bent over some round object and bound with tape for a day, which will give it the necessary "set" to ensure it sitting on the camber without any tendency to rise up at the sides, after which it can be glued and dowelled to the top frame of the house, and to the brackets extending out over the after end.

The margin-plank round the deck above is made from 1/8 in. x 1/16 in. mahogany and is glued and dowelled 1/16 in. in from the edge of the sycamore base, with the corners mitred of course. The planking is made from the same stuff as was used for the deck, but it should be rubbed down in thickness before use, so that when in position it will be 1/64 in. below the surface of the margin plank. Glue and dowel these planks in position, leaving the mast hole clear of course, and dowelling along the pencil lines representing the beams. The doors, if shown open, should be built of veneer, and for this I usually glue a piece of veneer to some stiff paper, then when the glue is dry, clean up the surface, after which the rails and stiles forming the door panels can be glued and dowelled in position, the external size of the door, including the framing, being larger than the finished job. Then when the glue is dry the whole can be polished, and only when that too is dry should the door be cut down to the required size, using a steel rule and a razor blade. The raw edges are then touched up with a fine brush. If the door is to be made to swing, then rub the paper off the reverse side and put the veneer rails and stiles on that too. The same will apply of course if the door is to be left half open so that both sides can be seen.

I did not attempt to provide any internal fittings, but gave the interiors of both houses a couple of coats of flat black, after which they were laid aside until required. The final fitting in the case of the forward house consisted of running some glue round the lower inside edged then pushing it down over the base fixed on deck, a couple of dowels in either end, driven home by means of a nail punch, completed the job.

The after house was built in the same way, but in this case the shell has to be made a push-fit inside the quarterdeck carlings, and in view of its very slightly curved sides, it is as well to fit a frame round both top and bottom inside, and perhaps make this from 1/4 in. square rather than 1/8 in. square. When the shell is complete push it in place and run a sharp pencil round the line of the deck, this will then form the bottom edge of the skirting of the panels. This skirting should be made of 1/32 in. mahogany, and the rest of the work from mahogany veneer. The completed skirting will hide the joint with the deck. The skylight was built of 1/32 in. mahogany on the same lines as the fo'castle companion, but the glazing was in perspex full length of the top and having the veneer frame fixed to it.

No attempt was made to fit the steering gear, instead this portion of the wheel-shelter was made as a solid block with a couple of 1/8 in. diameter dowels in the bottom to register with holes drilled in the deck. The house was then built round about this block using 1/32 in. sycamore for the shell and veneer for the panels. The doors were left open, and dowelled in that position, so the lavatory seat was fitted in one compartment and the "bench" of the store in the other. This house, too, was removed again when finished, and only glued to the deck when all the houses were put in place together.

On either side of the quarterdeck there are two timberheads which serve the same purpose as the bollards of a steel ship when in port, while at sea they are used to belay the two running parts of the main-sheet. These were made from 1/8 in. x 1/8 in. sycamore and have a round spigot formed in the end, which is glued into a hole in the deck, *Sketch No. 63.* The gallows and fife-rail require no explanation, for their construction will be perfectly clear from the *Sketch No. 78*, they are fixed by means of spigots in the deck, this fitting can also be made but not finally fixed.

We can now consider the hatch coamings, which in my model were made from 1/16 in. sycamore as shown in the *Sketch No. 79A.* A frame of this material was made, with the correct projection above the deck and deep enough to reach the bottom of the carlings. The whole thing was built carefully inside the square of the hatch and made with mitred corners, but before being glued each side was marked for deck level and the exposed portion French polished to a matt finish. Small metal "Z" cleats should be fitted at this stage too, a point which I overlooked, and then found it almost impossible to do anything about it when once the coamings were in position. I also left the coamings "natural" colour since that was to be the treatment for the whole ship, no paint being used anywhere. When the first frame has been fitted, make a second one to go inside it but leaving a ledge 1/16 in. down from the top to take the hatch covers. Glue the whole assembly in position, putting cross spars inside the hatch as wedges to ensure good contact with the beams and carlings, and when all is dry, skew-dowel each of the four sides.

Another form of hatch coaming common in small ships is that shown in *Sketch No. 79B*, and made in a model of the size of *Leon* from 1/8 in. square material, glued and dowelled to the deck, and having the corners mitred, after which a liner similar to that already described is fitted inside to provide the landing for the hatch covers. This type of coaming was however more likely to be found in smaller or older ships.

We have now reached the stage where it will be as well to fit the chain plates for the standing-rigging, although there is the alternative of leaving them off altogether for the present, and fitting them as required during the process of rigging. There is something to be said for both methods. They

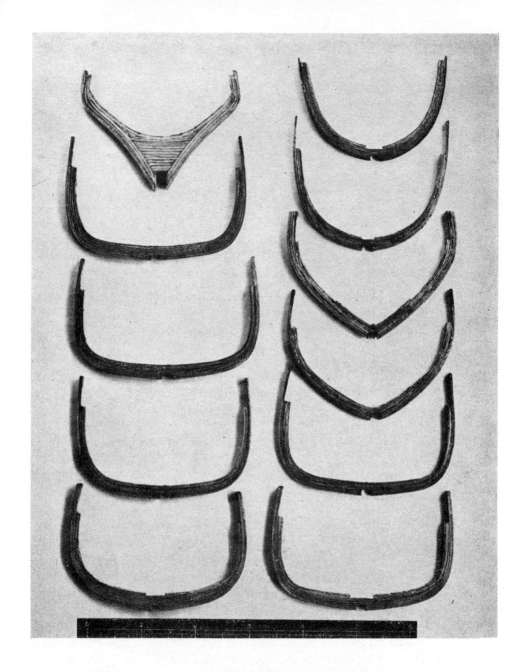

Fig. 21.
SMALL SCALE LAMINATED FRAMES READY FOR CLEANING UP.

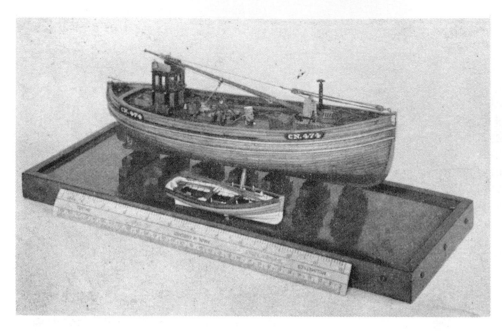

Fig. 22.

RING-NET FISHERMAN AND CLINKER- BUILT BOAT.
1/4 in. Scale Models by the Author.

Fig. 23

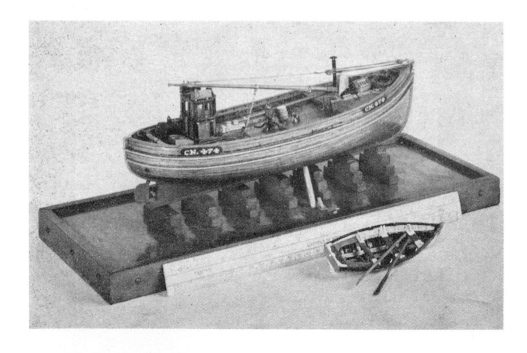

are more simple to fit at this present stage, on the other hand to be satis-factory they must run at the same angles as the rigging they serve. If fit-ted to the angles shown in the plans they will fair up with the backstays, etc., as designed, but the finished rigging does not always finish to quite the angles of the drawings. This in no way reflects on the builder, for it is surprising how very little is required to alter the angle of a stay. The mast the slightest bit out of rake, a bolster a fraction thicker than that intended in the design, or the eyes of the rigging facing a shade more fore or aft can make a difference to the angle that particular stay makes with the bul-warks. However, I think that on the whole it will be better to fit the chain-plates now.

The first job will be to make the dead-eyes, and in this much will depend upon the facilities the builder has available. If you have a lathe then the answer is obvious, if not then your draw-plate can come in handy, for you can rip down some lengths of box or sycamore and pull them through the plate to produce some rods of the required diameter, which can afterwards be parted off and rounded up by hand. Another alternative is to get some rods of ebonite of the required diameter and part these off in the required lengths. I made the dead-eyes from strips of boxwood cut from an old three-foot rule and drawn through the plate to the required diameter I then made a simple jig as shown in *Sketch No.* 80 for each size, which not only served for drilling the holes, but also for parting off. In view of the relatively few dead-eyes required, brass is quite hard enough for these jigs and is more easy to make than steel. I took a narrow strip of brass sheet and rolled it round the end of one of the boxwood sticks from which the dead-eyes were to be made, after which it was silver soldered along the butt. The ring so formed was then put down on a small piece of brass sheet and scribed round inside, after which the holes were drilled in the sheet and the ring soldered in place, and filed down to a depth equal to the thickness of the dead-eye.

In use I set a drill in the pin-chuck so that it projected a distance equal to the combined thickness of the dead-eye and brass plate, plus about 1/64 in., then the jig was placed on the end of the stick and the three holes drilled to the depth of the drill. The stick was then turned on its side and a saw cut run all round by means of a fine jeweller's saw held against the band. The stick was then withdrawn from the jig and the shallow groove for the strop filed all round, after which the edge of the saw cut was round-ed off, and finally the stick sawn right through to part off the eye. The drill will have marked the end of the stick from which the dead-eye has just been cut, but as this end has to be cleaned up again before it goes into the jig to make the next, the markings will disappear; it is all a matter of having the drill at the right length. The grooves for the strops were put in with a fine warding file, those for the dead-eyes in the rigging fairly deep,

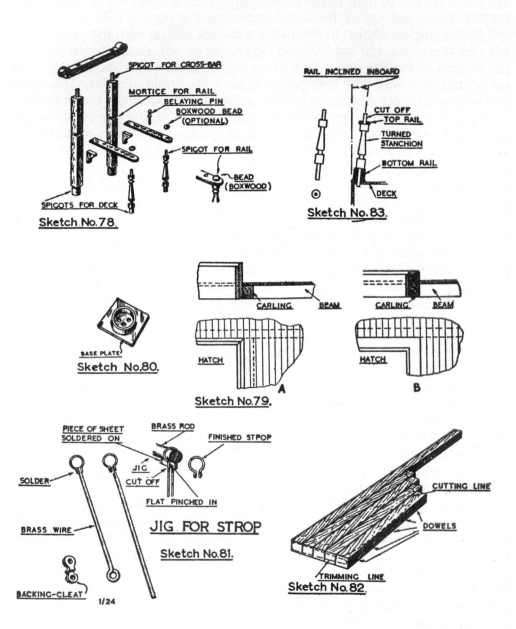

SPIGOT FOR CROSS-BAR

MORTICE FOR RAIL.
BELAYING PIN
BOXWOOD BEAD
(OPTIONAL)

SPIGOT FOR RAIL

BEAD
(BOXWOOD)

SPIGOTS FOR DECK

Sketch No. 78.

RAIL INCLINED INBOARD

CUT OFF
TOP RAIL
TURNED
STANCHION
BOTTOM RAIL.

DECK

Sketch No. 83.

BASE PLATE

Sketch No. 80.

CARLING   BEAM

HATCH   A

CARLING   BEAM

HATCH   B

Sketch No. 79.

PIECE OF SHEET
SOLDERED ON

BRASS ROD

FINISHED STROP

SOLDER

JIG
CUT OFF

FLAT PINCHED IN

BRASS WIRE

JIG FOR STROP

Sketch No. 81.

BACKING-CLEAT   1/24

CUTTING LINE

DOWELS

TRIMMING LINE
Sketch No. 82.

and the ones for the chain-plates shallow to allow the strop to spring into it as will be described.

I found that it was very easy to turn out dead-eyes quite quickly when once one got into the routine, and the finished job was quite satisfactory. Of course there is no reason why the dead-eyes should not be parted off before finishing, but I found it a great advantage to have them as part of the stick while rounding the ends and cutting the groove.

Like the dead-eyes themselves, the method of fixing to the chain-plates will largely depend upon the facilities available. Professor Favez made a proper job of his, drilling the strop and chain-plate and putting a pin through. At the time my model was built I had no tools for accurate repetition work such as this, so I devised the simplified version shown in *Sketch No.* 81, which on this scale looked quite satisfactory.

The fact that the chain-plates in this vessel were of round instead of flat bar simplifies matters considerably, and the first job will be to mark out the position and angle of the various chain-plates, then drill holes down througll the rail so that they just cut into the face of the top plank of the bulwarks, but without breaking it. I made the chain-plates of hard brass wire and slightly flattened the upper ends as shown. I then cut off a number of lengths of copper wire, long enough to form the strops of the particular size of dead-eye required, with a little to spare, and these I bent round a jig made of a piece of brass rod of the required diameter with a bit of brass sheet soldered on one side as shown in the sketch. The ends of the strops were pinched against this and the surplus cut off with the jeweller's cutters. These ends were then slipped over the flattened end of the chain-plate, and silver soldered. The finished strop was just big enough to be sprung over the end of the dead-eye and into the shallow score provided.

The chain-plate was then threaded down through the hole in the rail and the eye formed on the bottom by means of a pair of round-nosed pliers, and then finished off with the cleat, using small brass pins driven into the doublers already provided inside the hull. This is another job which I think I would do differently were I making another model of this ship, for I found the task of forming the lower eye in the wire needed great care if one was to avoid wrenching the rail and splitting it. I think it would he better to make the chain-plate complete, then cut a piece right out of the rail, to be replaced after all the plates were in position.

The rudder I built from 1/8 in. square material as in *Sketch No.* 82. This follows full-size practice yet involves no more work than cutting it out of one piece, in fact less of the kind of work I dislike. Take a length of 1/8 in. square material which will reach just up through the quarterdeck if you intend to make a working gear, (which I very much doubt on this scale), or to stop just short of the deck if you have built the wheel-shelter with a solid centre as I did. Now add another length to reach from the heel to the top of the blade, glueing and dowelling it in place, then a shorter piece and so on until the required width is reached. These may either be dowelled singly as they go on, or the whole may be glued and then dowelled right through. When the glue is dry the top and after edge can be filed to shape, while the sides are cleaned up until the forward edge is the same thickness as the stern-post, and the after edge slightly less. The fore edge and the stock should be rounded and the whole polished. The gudgeons and pintles I made from strips of copper cut off a bit of sheet, with the eyes and pins silver soldered in, these were then fixed in position by drilling holes right through the straps on both sides of the rudder—drilled from opposite sides to meet in the centre—and inserting lengths of copper wire, which were then cut off almost flush and lightly hammered up. The straps on the stern-post were fitted in the same way.

The shallow wash-strake round the anchor-deck is made from 1/8 in. x 1/16 in. material on edge, and may either go on plain or have a shallow groove scored along the outer face to form a moulding as shown in the plans. These wash-strakes should be bent on a jig before use, after which they must be fitted over the catheads and then glued and dowelled down on top of the capping-rail which runs round the edge of this deck. Another way to form this strake is to make it a little less in height and then add a small capping of veneer with a fractional overhang inside and out.

The timber rail round the quarterdeck will be the next job, and is one needing a little care. This rail is not perpendicular, but inclines inboard as shown in the plans, and consists of a 3/32 in. square rail along the deck, turned wood stanchions, and finally a light timber rail on top. The first job will be to make and fit the rail on deck, taking care to bevel the underside so that the outer face inclines to the angle required, as shown in *Sketch No.* 83. Next make the turned stanchions, which if you have a lathe will offer no difficulty, but as mine was not available I used the following method. I first cut off some strips of sycamore, then pulled them through the drawplate to produce round rods of the required diameter, these were then cut into suitable lengths and a cardboard template made of the exact length and shape of the finished stanchion, which was then "turned" in the breastdrill with the aid of warding files. A fairly long spigot was left on each end, and these were finally pushed into the draw-plate to reduce them to the exact diameter of the drill to be used for drilling the rails. I made a few extra stanchions in case of accidents, but as it turned out I did not need any of them, for the whole job went together without a single hitch.

The top rails were cut from 1/16 in. mahogany sheet, which was first glued down on a sheet of stout brown paper, then rubbed down to about 3/64 in. A template was made of the top of each of the lower rails, and from these the top rails were cut out, after which the positions of the stan-

SPACERS

SPARS TO BE RUBBED DOWN

B

FINISHED GRATING

C

A

SPARS GLUED TO PAPER

Sketch No. 84.

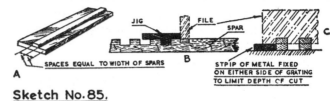

JIG   FILE   SPAR

C

A

SPACES EQUAL TO WIDTH OF SPARS

B

STRIP OF METAL FIXED
ON EITHER SIDE OF GRATING
TO LIMIT DEPTH OF CUT

Sketch No. 85.

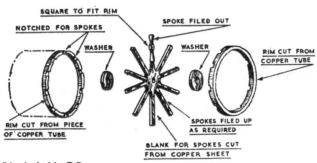

SQUARE TO FIT RIM

NOTCHED FOR SPOKES

WASHER

SPOKE FILED OUT

WASHER

RIM CUT FROM
COPPER TUBE

RIM CUT FROM PIECE
OF COPPER TUBE

SPOKES FILED UP
AS REQUIRED

BLANK FOR SPOKES CUT
FROM COPPER SHEET

Sketch No. 86.

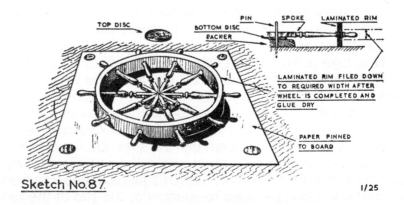

TOP DISC

PIN   SPOKE   LAMINATED RIM

BOTTOM DISC
PACKER

LAMINATED RIM FILED DOWN
TO REQUIRED WIDTH AFTER
WHEEL IS COMPLETED AND
GLUE DRY

PAPER PINNED
TO BOARD

Sketch No. 87.

1/25

chions were set out on these. The top rails were then laid along on the lower rails and held with adhesive tape while the holes for the spigots were drilled through both and well down into the deck below. The taff-rail had to be done separately because, owing to the inclination of the side stanchions, the upper rail across the stern is slightly shorter than the lower, although the stanchions are of course vertical.

When all was ready the lower spigots of the stanchions were coated with thin glue and pushed home in the holes provided, the top spigots were then glued and the top rail pushed in position, after which the surplus spigot above the rail was cut off and smoothed down. The joints between the side rails and taff-rail were re-inforced with a small piece of veneer on the underside.

That I think covers all the fittings required for this hull, except such odds and ends and the galley funnel and the cabin stove pipe. These I "turned"—in the breast-drill—from bits of brass rod, complete with cowl, but there is no reason why they should not be made from bits of brass tube if you have any of suitable size handy.

There are two small gratings in front of the wheelhouse, one on either side of the wheel, and these I made from strips of 1/16 in. square sycamore, cleaned down to a full 1/32 in. square. My method of making such gratings is quite simple, and all done by hand because I have no suitable machine tools for the work. The first stage is to take a sheet of paper and pin it down on a board, then cut off a number of strips of sycamore rather longer than the required grating, Take up the first strip and having glued it along one edge stick it down on the paper. Break off two short pieces of the material and glue these down one at either end of the long piece to act as distance pieces between it and the next spar. Take the next length and glue it down touching the distance pieces, add two more short bits at the end, followed by another long spar, and so on until the total area required by the grating is covered, at which stage your grating will appear as *Sketch No. 84A*.

Now take a flat straight edged warding file of the same thickness as the material being used, and half check all the spars by cutting across them with the file held against some form of straight-edge, making the spaces between the slots equal to the thickness of material being used. Now put a spot of glue in each half-check of one row, then take a length of sycamore and press it down into the slots. Do the same with the rest of the checks until all are used up, when the end view of your grating will appear as in *Sketch No. 84B*. Stretch a piece of fine sandpaper over a flat block of wood and proceed to sandpaper the top of the grating until the spars running in both directions are flush on top.

I made a very simple jig for cutting the half-checks, which in my opinion is well worth the little trouble required, particularly as it will always be available for making any future gratings of this scale which may be required. Take a strip of hard brass—steel would be better if you are likely to make a very large number of gratings—and on one side solder a straight strip of brass wire, the diameter of which should be the same as the breadth of the half-checks in the spars. The depth of these checks is of course half the breadth, so the surface of the wire will be filed down to this. Then file down one edge of the brass strip until it is the width of a spar away from the edge of the wire, and your jig will appear as *Sketch No. 85A*. In use you cut the first row of half-checks, then drop the wire of the jig into this row and use the edge of the brass strip as the guide for cutting the next row. Move the jig along to this row and use it to cut the next, and so on until all are cut, *Sketch No. 86B*. Another very useful guide is to pin a strip of metal, equal in thickness to half the thickness of the spars, along on either side of the grating when cutting the slots. These metal strips will prevent the file cutting the half-checks too deeply, *Sketch No. 86C*.

Having cleaned up the top of the grating it can be laid aside while the frame is made, for this I usually use either cedar or mahogany, which makes a nice contrast to the sycamore of the grating proper. On another piece of paper draw in the outside size of the complete grating, then the inside size of the frame, taking care when deciding this that it falls on the inside edges of a spar all round, otherwise you might find a spar running alongside the inner edge of the frame instead of a space. In other words the outside dimensions of the finished grating are governed by the size of space it has to occupy, while the inside sizes must be made in multiples of spars and spaces. Cut out the sides of the frame, mitre the ends and glue them down on the drawing and leave under a weight to dry, after which the paper inside the frame should be carefully cut away with a razor blade. Take the frame and set it down over the "rough" of the grating, mark all round the inside of the frame with a sharp pencil, then cut the grating to this with a razor blade without cutting the paper to which the grating is stuck. Carefully lift away the unwanted bits of the grating, and having put a spot of glue on the tips of the spars and on the underside of the frame, drop the latter over the grating and leave under a weight to dry. The face of the frame will of course have been cleaned up before cutting out the paper from the inside.

All that now remains is to clean up the face of the complete unit and polish it, after which it is rubbed on a sheet of sandpaper pinned down on a board, which will remove the paper from the underside, to be either polished or varnished as required. Where a grating has to be fixed down to the deck, or any other position where the underside will be obscured, I usually leave the paper on the back, merely cleaning out the holes between the spars with a fine square file, working from the underside of course to avoid any risk of damage to the upper surface, I then give the underside a coat of varnish on top of the paper. This ensures a strong joint between the frame and the spars.

Steering wheels can be something of a problem in ship models, and I have tried various methods of making them. The most simple method is perhaps that used in the Scandinavian barque model, where the wheel is all metal and painted. From the ever obliging junk-box I raised a bit of copper tube of just the right diameter for the rim, from this I cut two narrow "slices", making two rings each about half the width of the finished rim. Then from a sheet of copper of suitable thickness a "blank" was cut representing all the spokes in one piece. The two copper rings were halfchecked to take the spokes "blank", and a hole was drilled in the centre of what would ultimately be the boss of the wheel. The spokes were then filed up as required, after which the wheel was drawn down on a piece of wood and a "headless" nail driven in the centre as a pin on which to locate the spoke assembly. The inner faces of the copper rings were tinned—this model was built before I "discovered" silver soldering—they were placed in position on the circles drawn on the wood, and then sweated together with the spokes coming up between them. The wooden jig went on fire of course, but by that time the sweated joint was finished and rim and spokes were one. All that now remained was to insert the shaft in the hole in the centre, and sweat it up with a small brass washer on either side to form the hub, which was slightly loaded with solder to allow filing up. This model has a working gear, which was soldered to the other end of the shaft, the wheel itself being bound up in wet rag during the process, a precaution which would have been quite unnecessary with silver solder. *Sketch No. 86.*

If you have facilities for turning fine boxwood or sycamore spokes, then very good small wheels can be made using rims made from shavings, as will be described in Vol. II. for the mast-hoops. The boss can be turned from boxwood and drilled for the spokes, but a much better way in small wheels is to leave the ends of the spokes square and mitre them all together in the centre, *Sketch No. 87*, and form the boss from small wooden discs glued on the face, after which it can be drilled for the fixing pin. In making, leave the rim much wider than required, then slip it on a round stick which is a push fit inside, carefully mark out and drill the holes for the spokes, after which the rim can be removed from the stick. Having turned the spokes from suitable hardwood, set out the wheel on a piece of paper pinned down to a board. Glue the rim down on this, in its correct position. In the centre drive in an ordinary pin with the head cut off, and over this drop a small wooden disc and a packer, which must be just thick enough to form a landing for the spokes when pushed through the holes in the rim. The spokes will have to be inserted in the rim from the inside, but they will move outward until the square portion is against the hole, however it will not be necessary to move them as far as that. Feed the spokes carefully in to the central pin, trimming the corners of each with a razor blade until they all meet in a mitre at the central pin. Push them back and give the wooden disc a coat of thin glue, bring the spokes into position again, coat the underside of the second disc with glue and drop it in position, put a weight on top and leave to set. I should of course have mentioned that the spokes are also given a touch of glue where they pass through the rim, but that will be obvious. When the glue is dry the face of the rim can be filed down and polished while the wheel is still stuck down to the paper, after which it will be lifted and the paper cut away and the other side filed down in the same way. *Sketch No.* 87 shows this type of wheel under construction.

Lack of facilities for turning the spokes ruled out all forms of built wheel in the case of my *Leon* model, for while I managed to "turn" the rail stanchions in a breast-drill, this did not have the speed or accuracy necessary for turning the very fine spokes needed for a 1/8 in. scale model, so I had to revert to the very crude method of filing the wheel out of the solid. I had a broken bakelite cover off a motor car fuse panel, (in the junk-box of course!) and having split out a piece as large as needed I scribed the wheel on this, and then proceeded to drill and file it out. Seen through a fog or at a good long range the finished product is not too bad, but it is not exactly a fitting to which one particularly calls attention. However, it is really not very prominent, with the wheelhouse behind it and the after companion in front; it almost escapes notice, and in any case I console myself with the knowledge that I have seen worse in my time. At least it is not a nickel-plated abortion, and the colour is right and might well be mistaken for teak.

Another method of construction is to make the rim of a number of segments of wood, much as in the real thing, and on 1/4 in. scale or over this is quite possible. Cut a number of segments of wood and glue them down on a sheet of paper just as is done when making the mast collar, (Vol. II.), except that the number will be equal to the number of spokes in the wheel, and not four as shown in the drawing. The rim of the wheel is scribed on this, and cut out, while the spokes are made as in the wheel with the laminated rim made from a shaving, the only difference being that they will be square in section in way of the rim. Set out the wheel on paper and assemble the spokes, meeting in a common mitre at the centre as before, but this time glue them directly to the paper, and not to a wooden disc. Also glue the square portion of the spoke where it passes through the rim and fix this to the paper too. When the glue is dry, take up one of the segments of the rim and trim its ends until it will just rest between the spokes with its rim on the outer circle drawn on the paper below. When correct, glue its ends to the spokes on either side and glue it down to the paper too. Fit all the other segments of the rim in the same way, then clean up the surface. In a large scale wheel a brass ring should be cut and fixed to the face of the rim, while in smaller scale wheels this "brass" rim could be made of stout brown paper glued on. When one side is finished, clean the paper off the other and finish it in the same way.

The only thing which now remains to be done for the hull of our model is to decide on the external finish, which can either be paint, or as in my own model, French polish worked up to a matt finish. If you should intend to paint her, then use one of the thin paints made specifically for model work. I have no knowledge of her original colour scheme and can only give that of her later years. Up to 1909 she was sheathed with yellow metal below the line, but after that date it seems to have disappeared, perhaps because it had become in need of repair, which in view of the fact that by then her deep-water voyaging was probably over, was not considered worth the expense. The fact that she had been coppered at one time indicates that in her youth she had traded into warmer waters. After the copper disappeared she was given one of the anti-fouling coats below the line, and for the model either red or green would look the best, although it is probable that by the end of her days black would be more accurate, since tar is the cheapest of the lot. Above the line her colour in later years was grey, with white wash-strakes fore and aft. Everything inboard was then painted white, but it is probable that in her youth much of the panelled work would be bright varnished. All ironwork and hatch coamings were black, while the masts and spars were natural wood oiled, with the mastheads and the ends of all spars white, as can be seen in the photograph.

If the builder decides to copper the hull, now is the time to do it, but coppering is perhaps the most tedious of all jobs connected with the modelling of wooden ships. As my pleasure is largely derived from the building rather than the finished product, I confess that it is a job of which I fight shy if at all possible, and in the case of the plank-on-frame model I have invented an excellent excuse, namely that coppering hides the most interesting and pleasing part of the planking!

There really is a modicum of truth in this alibi, for the run of the copper sheets on a hull is arranged solely with an eye to saving wastage and labour in cutting sheets, resulting in three separate belts–Sketch No. 95–having little relation to each other and certainly not as pleasing to the eye as the flowing lines of the planking in the underwater body of a ship. Anyway, that is my excuse, and I am sticking to it!

Copper sheathing is fairly fine work on any scale, and particularly so on small models, so I think it will be as well to describe full-size practice, which will then allow the modeller to reproduce it as faithfully as his skill, facilities and scale will permit.

The copper was supplied in sheets 4 ft. 0 in. long and from 15 in. to 18 in. wide, and was put on the hull on top of a layer of tarred felt. In model work a suitable adhesive can be substituted for the felt, and will reinforce the minute pins which otherwise would be solely responsible for fixing the sheets, The longitudinal joints were lapped clinker fashion, i.e. each strake overlapping the one immediately below, while the vertical joints had the lap facing aft, so that the movement of the ship through the water did not tend to lift the edges of the sheets. All laps were joggled, the copper being hammered down on to the hull right up to the edge of the sheet to be over-lapped, then the lap was hammered down and nailed.

Stem, stern-post and keel were plated with sheets running length-wise along them, the side sheets being turned down round the outer faces, and the underside of the keel, all of which were then covered by a wrapper plate extending down the front of the stem, along the bottom of the keel and up the after edge of the stern-post, put on in 4 ft. 0 in. sec-tions of course. The rudder was plated in horizontal strakes, the fore and aft edges being treated like those of the stem and stern-post.

To keep the vertical laps running correctly all plates must be laid from the stern forward, so the first plate to go on will be that at the junction of the stern-post with the keel. Work forward along either side of the keel, and when this is plated fore and aft, the sides of the stern-post should be covered, followed by the plates down the after edge of the latter.

There are several ways of arriving at the run of the strakes on the hull proper, all resulting in much the same arrangement in the end, namely three belts of copper each comprised of a number of strakes of uncut full-width sheets. Goring belts, (B) and (E) in *Sketch No.* 95, with certain sheets cut as necessary, fill the spaces left between the other three. The methods of arriving at this layout differed in different yards, although the only real difference in the final result was a matter of the number of strakes in the respective belts. The following method has the advantage of being simple to work, although the builder can vary the number of strakes in different belts if he wishes.

Start from the keel at the stern-post and run a strake of plating right forward to the stem, using full-width sheets without cutting, then follow this with another strake laid in the same way, but with the vertical joints stag-gered of course. The fact that these strakes are of full width throughout will mean that at their ends they will rise steeply up the stem and stern-post respectively, but continue adding such strakes until their ends reach any-thing from one-third to one-half the distance from the keel to the waterline. This belt will then be as the shaded section (A) in the sketch.

From the top ends of this belt at stem and stern-post run a batten round the hull so that it rests fair all along, striking a pencil line along the hull at its lower edge. This will be line (Y) on the sketch and will cross the midship frame about the turn of the bilge, leaving a gap between it and the lower belt, tapering to either end as shown. The space between this line and the copper already fixed represents the first goring belt as indicated by the unshaded section (B) in the sketch.

This goring belt is now fixed by running strakes of full-width uncut sheets along the top of the belt (A), but cutting the tops of the end sheets to the line (Y) drawn on thc hull. Continue adding full width strakes in the same way until the whole of the open space between belt (A) and the line (Y) is filled, with all the end plates cut off flush with that line.

Now move up to what is to be the top edge of the finished coppering, usually 9 in. to 12 in. above the load waterline, and run a pencil line right round the hull at this level and parallel to the waterline—Line (C.L.) on the sketch. From this line measure down the hull a distance equal to two or three—according to the size of the ship—full-width strakes of copper, and strike in another line, (X) in the sketch, at this level and again parallel to the waterline. This represents the lower edge of the top straight belt. (C).

All is now ready for running the next parallel belt, shaded and marked (D) on the sketch. This is run as before, in full-width sheets with the first strake overlapping the goring belt (B) along line (Y). Continue adding full-width strakes until their top corners reach the line (X) at stem and stern-post, which means that the hull is now plated up to the level of the line (Z) on the sketch.

Goring belt (E) follows next and is made up exactly as belt (B), full-width plates being run parallel to belt (D) but with the ends cut off to an angle so that they finish along line (X).

All that now remains is to run belt (C) in full-width sheets as before, the lower strake lapping the goring belt (E) along the line (X). Add as many strakes as has been allowed for to bring the plating up to the required level, line (C.L.), after which the stem sides can be plated, finishing with the wrapper plate down the forward edge of the stem and along the under-side of the keel, and the job is complete, by which time, if you have been working with scale size sheets, you will have driven about 13,000 very small pins to fasten the copper, and probably lost about an equal number on the floor! The finished effect will be seen in the unshaded side of the sketch.

The best material for coppering a model is hard rolled copper-shim, from l/l000 in. to 3/1000 in. thick and obtainable from most merchants dealing in non-ferrous metals.

When the hull has received its final treatment, the various houses and fittings can be fixed in position and we are all ready for the next important stage, the making of the masts and spars or if you wish, the finished stand and case although I usually leave that until the model is complete.

However this is a good point to say something about the mounting of the model, since provision for this should be made while the hull is easy to handle and before it is rigged. I am not going to attempt to offer any advice on the subject of making glass cases, for it is a job I have never undertaken except for small models where the frame can be made of a light "L" section wood which one used to be able to obtain from most hobby shops. For the larger models I have either dispensed with a case and kept them in the open, or as with *Leon* and *Buteshire*, I have had the case made for me by a firm of shop fitters.

The question of the type of stand to be used is one for the builder, it may either take the form of a polished plinth with the model supported on metal pedestals as illustrated by Professor Favez's model, or on blocks as would be found in a shipyard, which is the method I use if the job is to go into a case. Both the Scandinavian barque and the barquentine in *Fig.* 12 a wartime casualty by the way, and no longer in existence—are in simple cradles, really intended merely to support the model during rigging, but never replaced by anything better.

If the model is to be mounted on metal pedestals, then provision must be made for bolts to go down through the keel, for while the top of the pedestal may grip the keel sufficiently to hold the model firm under steady conditions, I think one must always allow for the case being moved from place to place. With a laminated or solid hull the holding-down bolts can be screwed straight in, but with a "built" hull I think they should go right through keel and keelson and be fixed with a nut and washer on top. In a small scale model such as *Leon* this may mean fitting doublers alongside keel and keelson in way of the bolts, or if the bolts are kept small enough to go through the scale keel then I would fit additional pedestals under each bilge, although these need not have any direct connection to the hull, since their function would be merely to prevent the model trying to fall to one side or another in event of the case being tilted.

With the model raised up on keel-blocks the matter is more simple, for one can always fit some "props" under the bilges to steady the model, just as would be done in a shipyard. I usually make these props from natural twigs or small branches, collected well in advance—as soon as I have decided to start a model in fact—so that they will be well seasoned by the time they are required. Sometimes I leave the bark on the props, in which case I clean it off for about 3/8 in. from the bottom, drill a hole in the base to take this and glue it in, so that there is no risk of the prop coming adrift no matter how much the case is moved about. The top of each prop is cut a little short of the underside of the model, then with the model held in place, small wedges, glued on the underside, are pushed between the top of the prop and the underside of the hull, then when the glue has dried the model is lifted off and each wedge dowelled into the top of the prop.

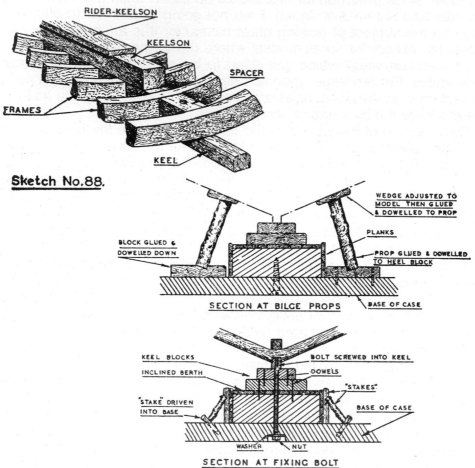

RIDER-KEELSON

KEELSON

SPACER

FRAMES

KEEL

Sketch No. 88.

WEDGE ADJUSTED TO MODEL THEN GLUED & DOWELLED TO PROP

BLOCK GLUED & DOWELLED DOWN

PLANKS

PROP GLUED & DOWELLED TO HEEL BLOCK

SECTION AT BILGE PROPS

BASE OF CASE

KEEL BLOCKS

BOLT SCREWED INTO KEEL

INCLINED BERTH

DOWELS

"STAKES"

"STAKE" DRIVEN INTO BASE

BASE OF CASE

WASHER   NUT

SECTION AT FIXING BOLT

Sketch No. 89.

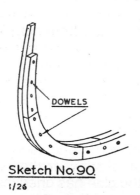

DOWELS

Sketch No. 90.

1/26

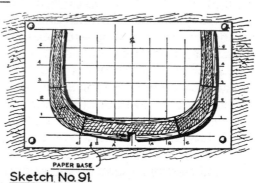

PAPER BASE

Sketch No. 91.

For connecting the model to the keel-blocks I either use simple locating pins made from brass wire, the upper end with a fine thread cut on it and screwed into the wood of the keel, the other being plain to slip into a hole in the keel-blocks. With this arrangement the model will remain fixed through all reasonable handling of the case, yet it can be lifted off the stand at any time if required. The model of the ring-net boat seen in some of the photographs is mounted in this way.

A number of years ago I bought a quantity of brass rod of various gauges, in about 12 in. lengths and screwed a B.A. thread throughout the length, some of which I used in the *Leon* model, *Sketch No.* 89. After the keel-blocks were all laid I drilled right down through two sets of them and out through the base of the case. I drilled two corresponding holes in the keel of the model and into each of these I screwed one of the finer sizes of rod, leaving it to cut its own thread in the wood. The model was then placed in position on the blocks and the rods cut off to length, which was just sufficient to leave them in recessed holes on the underside of the base of the case. A brass washer was slipped over each rod, followed by a brass nut which was pulled up tight, after which a little putty closed the recessed holes, locked the nuts, and yet leaves a means of getting at them again at some future date should the need arise. The brass rods used are very light so there was no need to double the keel at these points, but they are amply strong enough to prevent the model rising off the blocks during handling the case, which is all that is required of them, for the duty of keeping the model upright is carried out by the four bilge-props. These were fitted slightly dilferently to the method used on previous models, for instead of being sunk in holes in the base I fitted their heels into checks in "strong horizontal bulks of timber intended to spread the weight of the hull over a larger area of ground". The props are glued to the "bulks" and dowelled up through the bottom, after which the "bulks" were glued and pinned to the base. The props were made a little short, and wedges fitted on top to get exactly the right contact with the hull. These too are glued and dowelled. Such props would of course be found in the full-size yard, although they would extend at fairly close intervals all along the hull, while there would also be further props from higher up the ship's side. I did at one time think of putting in the full number, but decided against it since much of the pleasure to be obtained from looking at the ship's lines would have been lost, instead I merely provided sufficient to give the model a stable stand, in which it would be safe against all reasonable tilting of the case in the event of it being moved from one building to another.

The actual berth is inclined, and its sides are shored up with very rough timbering and planks, all just "spiked" together with very obvious and very roughly driven "spikes". The struts supporting the timbering are also of very rough material, with their heels against stakes driven into the "ground". On the port side of the berth there is a pile of unbarked "logs" (all duly glued and pinned of course to prevent movement), while to starboard there is a pile of finished material for replanking the hull, this is stacked with cross members at intervals to ensure "proper ventilation". Two or three ladders just "kicking about" (in appearance, but not in fact), a staging on trestles aft, with two men caulking a scam, the shipyard "boss" and a few more men completes the make-up so far, but I hope in time to add the anchors and cables laid out for inspection; the boat being either painted or repaired. There is no "spit-and-polish" about this berth, and I am afraid it would not please some people, but I like "atmosphere" if I can get it, and my only regret is that I veneered and polished the actual base, but I will probably glue and sand it when I make another start on the model, in any case there are still a few "rat-tails" in the rigging to be cut away, but I did not notice them until after the photographer had gone away. The shipyard workers, which also help to convey the scale of the model, I carved from small pieces of sycamore.

However, providing the reader decides just how he intends to fix his model to the base when finished, and makes the necessary provision before it is too late, he need not worry any more about the final set up, leaving that to be the very last job. For the purpose of rigging, some form of small cradle or stand which can be turned this way and that with ease is the best, since in the actual process of rigging, which will be covered in detail in Vol. II., one is working continuously from side to side, and a large stand just gets in the way. The simple stand on which my own *Leon* was rigged is shown in *Fig.* 17.

Fig, 24.
Finished Model.

1/2 in. SCALE MODEL OF ZULU *MUIRNEAG*.
(Now in National Maritime Museum, Greenwich).
By M. George McLeod, Stornaway.

Fig. 25.
Partly decked, showing
bunks etc., in cabin.

Fig. 26.
Mr. McLeod's Zulu under construction and
Frame-jig showing in use.

Fig.27.
Dr. K Tulloch's Motor Fishing Vessel
(See Volume II)

CHAPTER VI

A FEW ALTERNATIVES IN FRAME MAKING

WITH the hull now complete, we can sit back and take stock of it, and perhaps consider what changes of method we will make when building the next one, for having once started on plank-on-frame construction, there is almost certain to be a "next". So it is that I think this a good point to have a look at some of the alternatives which can be used in that "next" hull.

In the previous chapters I have assumed that the builder wanted to follow the real thing as closely as possible on a small scale and with the facilities available to the man who has only the "kitchen table" type of workshop, although for myself, even though I changed my green-baize table for a more elaborate workshop, I would make very little change in the method of building, although I would of course have better equipment for doing the same jobs. The model so far described might be regarded as in the middle range as far as accuracy goes. It could get nearer to the prototype by adding such things as hanging-knees, ceiling in the hold, and fully framing all houses on deck. On the other hand what work has gone into the hull—excepting the houses—has been a scaled-down version of full-size practice, any departures from that have been faults—if that is not too strong a word—faults of omission not commission, and to produce a really accurate fully detailed scale version of a wooden ship, all the reader needs to do is to add those little extras as shown in the sections of full-sized craft which are used in this book. The workmanship involved will in no way differ from that already described.

I have already shown how the properly jointed frame, using butt-chock and scarfed joints, can be made by the same methods, but this does not altogether exhaust the alternatives available to the "true-to-prototype" builder, while there are also some simplified methods which may appeal to the man who is interested only in the external appearance of the finished product, without caring very much how that effect has been obtained, the man for whom the result and not the making is the primary consideration.

In *Leon* the frames are single with a more or less equal space between each, but perhaps the more common arrangement was to build the frames in pairs as shown in *Sketch No.* 25. Each frame, or timber to use its proper term, is of the same scantlings whether single or double, while there will be the same number of frames in the hull, the only difference is that two frames are built side by side, and the space between each pair opened up accordingly, so that the rule of "room and space" still applies as shown in *Sketch No.* 1. The double frame has much to recommend it to the model builder, since it can offer a simplified form of construction, yet one which is very near to full-size practice, particularly in the field of smaller and later day ships, such as fishing craft and small coasters, and also quite representative of the big ship too. However let us first consider the preliminary work required on the drawings to make them suitable for double frame construction, whether carried out with pairs of fully jointed frames or a simplified type.

With the single timber we ruled two lines across the Half-breadth Plan at every frame station, one representing the fore and the other the after side of the timber, whereas for double-timbers three lines will be required, representing the fore and aft faces of the pair, and the joint between them. The spacing of the frame stations will also be increased as already explained. The method of taking the shapes of the timbers from the Lines Plan and introducing the necessary drawings on which they will be formed, will of course be the same, but whether you produce one or two drawings for each pair of frames will largely depend upon the scale of the model and the type of construction being used. If the model is to be to a fairly large scale, or the frames are to be made with the scarfed or butt-chock joints as previously described, then it will be necessary to treat each frame of the pair as a separate unit, each to be built on its own constructional drawing, and only glued and dowelled together after completion, including cutting the bevels. The really important point is that after the bevels have been cut on each frame of the pair, the meeting faces should be identical when brought together, a very ready proof of the care you have taken in cutting your frames! In working out the run of the grain in each frame of a pair, it is very necessary to see that the futtocks are arranged differently in each unit, as shown in *Sketch No.* 25. This however is not difficult if strips of card are used as previously suggested. The job is simplified by the fact that only one frame of the pair has a floor running across the keel, the other one starts with a futtock on either side and a joint on top of the keel.

Going back to the same sketch, it will be seen that in full-size practice the two frames are locked against any tendency to "creep" on the joining faces by means of "joint-dowels", which are in effect square pegs fitting into matched mortices cut in the faces of adjoining frames. In model work these can be replaced by dowels right through the pair of frames at these points, but in a fore-and-aft direction, locking the pair together. These dowels will of course be fitted after the frames have been glued.

That covers the prototype construction of double frames, but for the builder who wants a simplified form, then that shown in *Sketch No.* 90 probably supplies the answer, for in this there is no need for the scarfed or butt-chock joints, instead, each half of the double frame serves as the jointing member for the other. One disadvantage of this is that one cannot set out the bevel at three different stations as in the other type, since the two halves cannot be formed separately. The general procedure is much the same, first set out the frame stations on the Lines Plan, but treat them as having double the normal sided width, showing on the plan only those lines which will represent the two outer faces of the complete unit. Make your small working drawing as before, showing both internal and external outlines for both faces, as illustrated in *Sketch No.* 29, and when finished pin this drawing, which has been made on tracing paper of course, face down on a board. Now saw out a series of "roughs" which will entirely cover the outlines seen up through the tracing paper, to which they are then glued as in *Sketch No.* 91. Next cut another series of "roughs", with joints overlapping and glue them down on top of the first, then put a sheet of paper on top to prevent them sticking to the weight under which they should be left until dry.

While these are drying the next pair can be taken in hand, then when the first pair can be handled they should be dowelled together as shown in *Sketch No.* 90, after which the surplus paper can be cut away, then the frame sawn out to the outer lines, and finally bevelled to the inner ones; the paper can then be cleaned off both sides and the frame is ready for the final polish. There is quite a lot to be said for this method, for it simplifies fitting by omitting all the "fancy" joints, and the square butt joint, such as that made by this type of frame, was in quite common use, Although in the larger ships it was usual to end-dowel each futtock as shown in *Sketch No.* 26B, but once in place, this dowel could not be seen. There is no question about the strength of this type of frame, its only real disadvantage is the fact that the bevel cannot be cut so accurately, and one has double the thickness to saw through when cutting out the frame from the "rough".

Another form of frame which can be used in hulls of certain types in the bent or steamed frame, but as that is more applicable to working models I do not propose to say any more about it here, for it will be fully covered in Vol. II.

Plate No. 4 is the constructional plan for a model built on the "cut-out-in-one-piece" form of frame making, and therefore makes no claim to being of prototype construction. Of course such a model can still be 100 per cent. perfect externally, providing that no planks are omitted from the hull or deck. This model has one great fault however, the frames are much too widely spaced, and to make a really good job, even externally, it would be as well to run some light bent frames between the sawn-out frames, just to allow for the necessary external fastenings; this however is a simple matter and I used it in the model shown in the photograph *Fig.* 4.

The drawing from which *Plate No.* 4 has been taken was made for a model which I built many years ago, but which never got past the bare hull stage and is still knocking about the office waiting for its first coat of polish or varnish—which it is never likely to get now! I do not propose to go into detail regarding this model since the construction will be obvious from the plan, but I may perhaps mention that the frames were sawn out, complete with deck beams, from 1/4 in. thick sycamore, and in spite of the fact that certain parts of all frames must be in cross-grain, there has been no sign of fracture anywhere, but with this wood it is sometimes difficult to decide just which way the grain does run, and there is little difference in strength either way.

The chief difference between this model and my later efforts is that I then cut the various units from the solid whenever possible, whereas now I prefer to build up from small pieces. Perhaps the fact that I was full 30 years younger when I built that model may have had something to do with the reckless expenditure of labour in sawing out all that material, but I prefer to think that the real explanation is that I am now 30-odd years wiser and therefore fully appreciate the better value of the built-up frame, both as to the pleasure to be obtained from making it and the knowledge when finished that the result is nearer to the real thing. I do not claim that it means less work, but it certainly is lighter work, and that to me means quite a lot! The methods of setting out the frames, finding the run of the planking are of course the same for either form of construction.

If the reader wants to reduce the planked model to its most simple form, then stem, keel and stern-post can be cut out as a single plank, which will extend up to the underside of the deck. Into this plank steps will be cut for the masts, while the frames will be replaced by solid bulkheads half-checked into the centre backbone as shown in *Sketch No.* 92. The external appearance of such a model is much the same as that of the fully built one, but in my view the pleasure of building is completely lacking and for that reason it is a type of construction which does not appeal to me.

There is another form of frame which can be used where internal details are not regarded as being of great importance, although the general principle of the fully-framed model is followed. This is the laminated frame, which I have used in one or two small models, but I see no reason why it should not also be applied on a slightly larger scale. Up to the time I first used it, it was entirely new to me, although of course it may have been used before. In my case it was a matter of "necessity being the mother of invention", for at the outbreak of World War II., I was stationed in Scapa Flow, a location which, as all who served there will remember, did not exactly overflow with supplies of any kind other than those of war. For the first few months we were all kept busy and the "off duty" period was almost unknown, but when things began to settle into normal service routine, the odd periods of relaxation became a little more frequent and my thoughts at such times turned to the subject of models. Materials however were obviously going to be a problem, and tools almost nil, but something had to be done, and in the end I managed to make a small "corner" in the supply of wooden "spills", or pipe-lighters, by getting all and sundry to buy for me in the various canteens. I now at least had some "timber", not very promising stuff I had to admit, but at least it was something, and as a matter of fact when I had time to quietly examine my stock I found that each bundle was a very mixed bag. Much of it was very rough stuff which I immediately placed in the category of "consumable stores" and returned to the purpose for which it had been intended, namely lighting pipes, but in the remainder there was a fair proportion of good material, obviously produced from the waste ends of such timber as teak, walnut, mahogany, cedar, etc.

These "spills" are of course about 1/32 in. thick, 1/4 in. wide and perhaps 5 in. long, and appeared very limited in their application to the craft of shipbuilding. However, I wrote home for a few tubes of adhesive "just in case", and shortly afterwards made one or two small clinker-built boats and a Loch Fyne Skiff, all of which will be mentioned in Vol. II., and some of which survived to find a place in my office today, although others were begged by friends.

One day I was sitting on the bulwarks of a drifter watching some men repairing the old wooden pier at Lyness, when the end sawn off a pile came floating by, and being a regular magpie where timber is concerned, I fished it out and added it to the rest of my "stores" although at that time I could not see any possible use for a piece of end-grain greenheart about 14 in. square and 4 in. deep. As a matter of fact it proved a fine block on which to work when making the small open boats, but later it was to form the basis of my idea for building a model ship, even though the only material available was in short strips little thicker than veneer. However the idea began to take shape, and the next job was to beg a handful of steel panel pins from the civilian contracting firm which was building huts in the shore base. My shipyard was now complete, both as to material and equipment, and all that remained was to get the drawing office functioning. Of course I had no plans, but I produced a set of Lines on a sheet of squared paper misappropriated from my Service stock, and as no tracing paper was available, from this I made a separate drawing of each frame, using a piece of carbon paper face up below the drawing, so that it was reproduced on both sides.

The drawing of the midship frame was pinned down on the block of greenheart and I was all set for my new experiment in making ship's frames from pipe lighting spills. The greenheart block was of course end-grain, and this is very important, for it allowed the panel pins to be driven into it *exactly* where required, whereas when I tried driving them exactly on the line of a drawing pinned on a normal piece of board, they always found the softer places between the grain and wandered slightly. But there I am getting a little ahead of my story.

With the drawing of the frame pinned down on the block, I proceeded to drive a steel "wall" of panel pins all round the outer line of the frame, as shown in *Sketch No.* 93, placing them as close together as possible, each pin touching the next, also taking care that the face and not the point of the pin was on the line. The fact of the block being end-grain will make this possible. The "wall" started about 1/2 in. above the top of the frame on one side, and ran right round to the same distance above the top on the other, so that I now had a metal jig of the external shape of the frame. The next job was to select suitable "spills" from my collection and cut them down to the required sided width of the proposed frame, using a razor blade with a table knife as a straight-edge. When I had a supply available I took up the first piece and pressed it round the inside of the jig, taking care that the lower edge rested on the pencil line indicating the side of the mortice for the keel. Then another strip was coated with adhesive on one side and pressed home on top of the first, after which these two were held in close contact with the jig by means of ordinary pins pushed into the base behind them. Two strips were then fixed on the other side of the keel mortice, and so I continued adding a strip at a time until the full depth of the mortice was reached, after which the laminations were carried right across and up both sides of the frame, until the floor on top of the mortice was of the required thickness. The reduction in the moulded size of the frame as it neared the top was made by cutting each lamination a fraction shorter than the one before it, taking care that the pencil line representing the inside of the frame was just covered all the time. The upper part of the frame was carried a little beyond the proper finishing line, which ensured the true sweep of the topsides being carried all the way. When sufficient laminations were on, the inside of the frame was held firmly in position by a row of ordinary pins driven almost "shoulder to shoulder" against the inner laminations, and left for the adhesive to set.

When everything was dry all pins were removed—both panel and ordinary—and one face of the frame cleaned up with sandpaper, after which the surplus paper was cut away from the edges of the frame, which was then bevelled to the inner line of the drawing still adhering to the other side. I found that the most useful tool for cutting the bevel was a nail file,

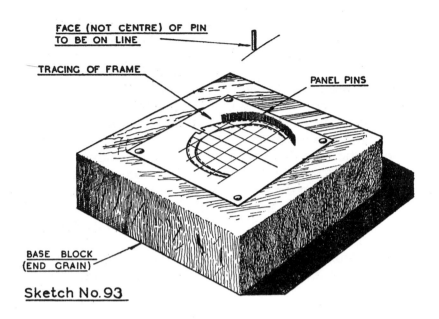

FACE (NOT CENTRE) OF PIN
TO BE ON LINE

TRACING OF FRAME

PANEL PINS

BASE BLOCK
(END GRAIN)

Sketch No. 93

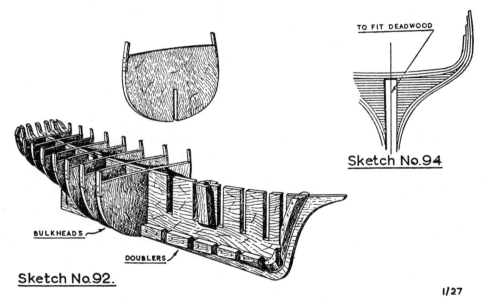

TO FIT DEADWOOD

Sketch No. 94

BULKHEADS

DOUBLERS

Sketch No. 92.

1/27

but I do not suggest that this be used if a more normal implement is available!

As soon as the first frame was removed from the jig another drawing was pinned down and a new jig formed of panel pins, and so on until a full set of frame's had been made. Where frames required a deep mortice to go over the top of the deadwood, or were too steep off the keel to go across it, the first one or two laminations were made to follow the shape of the frame, after which the space between them was filled in with horizontal laminations to form a deep floor and then the last two swept up into the run of the frame again, *Sketch No.* 94.

In this model the keel had to be fabricated from wood out of a cigar box, while the stem followed the same construction as the frames and was laminated, as were the beams. Some little time ago I started building another small model on the same principle, a few of the frames of which are shown in the photograph *Fig.* 21. The laminations in this case have been cut from some old veneer which I happened to have by me, and therefore go right round the frame in one piece—except for the keel mortice of course. These are still in the rough, ready for sandpapering but they give an idea of the result.

This particular method of construction will of course have its limitations, since the panel pins forming the jig would not be strong enough for heavy material, but I think it would be workable for models up to about 20 in. or 30 in. in length, providing that the laminations were made of thin material, say about 1/32 in. thick, certainly not more than 1/16 in. When one had a choice of material the laminations would of course be carried right round the frame in one piece, in my own case I had to be content with about 5 in. because that was all I could get at that time.

There are still further applications of the laminated frame, in the field of the sailing model, for example, where it would probably prove quite a good job. The method of construction would be exactly as that to be described in Vol. II., except that instead of bending the frame round the mould in one thickness, it would be laid on in two or possibly three laminations, which would be very easy to bend and, when once the dowels holding the planks were in, exceedingly strong.

Plates No. 5, 6, 7 are detailed construction plans of the Scottish Zulu type fishing vessel *Muirneag* of Stornoway, and are part of a complete set of 1/2 in. scale drawings which I produced in collaboration with Mr. George McLeod of Stornoway, who made the survey of the vessel just prior to her being broken up. Mr. McLeod also followed the process of breaking up, which enabled many of the normally inaccessible constructional details and fastenings to be examined and drawn on paper, and it is from these drawings that he built the perfect model illustrated in the photographs, *Figs.* 24 *to* 26, a model which has since been acquired by The National

Maritime Museum, Greenwich.

I have included these plans and photographs for several reasons, first the model itself is a beautiful example of craftsmanship in general and the framed model in particular, a model in which all the constructional features have been faithfully reproduced even though the hull has been planked over. Not only is the timbering complete and the planking perfect, but as will be seen from some of the photographs taken in the early stages of construction, so are the furnishings of the fish hold and cabin, where the seat-lockers and framing of the bunks show between the beams in one picture. In fact this model is the old *Muirneag* shrunk by some form of magic to 1/2 in. scale. These photographs are of interest in that they illustrate one or two features already mentioned in reference to other models, as for example the use of a top jig for locating the frames during construction, and the lodging-knees in the angles between beams and carlings. This model confirms a pet theory of mine, namely that there is far more pleasure in building a large scale model of a small vessel, than a small scale model of a large one, since it is possible on the larger scale to follow shipyard practice, and every small component is a model in itself.

This model also has the advantage of being built by a man who has himself spent much of his early life at sea under sail in just such craft, and therefore knows his subject inside out. It was this practical knowledge which was of such assistance in the survey of the ship. Mr McLeod has since surveyed other disappearing types of Scottish fishing vessel, and we hope to fully detail those too, while to that I add my own personal hope that when those drawings are available Mr. McLeod will allow himself to be persuaded to put them into model form.

The plans of the *Zulu* are of interest in showing still further methods of framing a wooden hull, as applied to small craft, small that is in comparison to the square-riggers so far described. It will be noted that in the midship body only every second frame extends right down to the keel, the others being floating frames running up from the garboard strake. The frames which do go right through are connected across the keel by heavy floors into which they are scarfed. In the ends of the ship there are floors at every frame, but instead of the latter being scarfed into them they are bolted on to the face, forward in the fore body and aft at the stern. All these types of frame will be seen in the various cross sections, which also show that this vessel followed big ship practice in having very short sections scarfed into the heads of all frames for easy replacement in case of damage, in fact the scarfs are only about two strakes below the deck line. The bow and stern show the use of the apron as forming part of the rabbet for the planking, in the bow for example the bevel of the rabbet is on the after side of the stem proper, so covering the hood-ends of the planks, a construction which could be followed with the stem and stern-posts of the

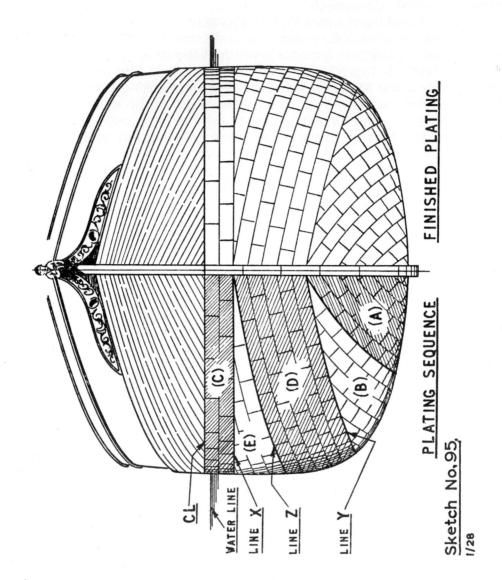

FINISHED PLATING

PLATING SEQUENCE

Sketch No. 95,

1/28

CL

WATER LINE

LINE X

LINE Z

LINE Y

(A)

(B)

(C)

(D)

(E)

brigantine. There is no gripe-piece, for like *Leon* she has a very sharp fore-foot, but in this case the stem and keel are halved and through bolted. The rabbet of the keel is formed by the junction between the keel and keelson, another feature which can be copied in model work for vessels other than the *Zulu*, in fact there is a great deal to be learned from a close inspection of the constructional details of this vessel.

APPENDIX I

SUMMARY OF CONTENTS OF VOLUME II

MAKING scale masts and spars, with description of full-size practice. Making scale "ironwork" and fittings for masts and spars of wooden vessels: Construction of tops, cross-trees, and other details: Masting jigs: Setting up the masts and bowsprit, the use of mast wedges in model work: Block-bulls-eye and fairlead making: Preparation of rigging materials: Tools for model rigging work: Standing-rigging, full-size and model practice: Serving, splicing, and making strops and grommets in model work: Running-rigging, with lead and belaying of gear: Rigging jigs: Tables of relative sizes of standing and running gear: Belaying-pin layout and table: Table of all rigging in model of brigantine *Leon*: Chain making, plain and stud-link: Light hulls for sailing models: Bent-frame construction: Sawn-out frame construction: Clinker-building for small craft: A few notes on sailing models and ballast: A simple steam chest: Photographs of model square-riggers under sail, clinker-built boats, and types of power craft: Plans and many drawings and sketches of constructional and rigging details.

APPENDIX II

SAILING SHIP DRAWINGS

THE publishers can supply sets of sailing ship plans specially drawn by the Author to scales suitable for model construction, and consisting of Lines Drawing; General Arrangement Drawing with Deck Plans; Sail and Rigging Plan including all running-rigging, and, in certain cases, additional sheets providing scale details of individual deck fittings, masts, spars, rigging, etc.

The aim of these drawings is to provide authentic data for those interested in the sailing ship period, or desiring to build models of named ships. They are based on original drawings and specifications, from which all essential information has been condensed into three or more sheets of convenient size.

With a view to illustrating the ship as she actually went to sea, the original details have been edited as far as possible by personal survey of such vessels as were available, from the author's own records and research work, or both, but the author will always be pleased to learn of any changes which, through lack of information, may not have been embodied or noted on the drawings, so that such information can be added.

The undermentioned ships are at present available, together with a few sets for the construction of simple models not intended to represent any particular vessel.

Acamas. — Steel full-rigged ship. A large modern ship rigged vessel of 1860 tons.

Admiral Karpfanger. — Four masted barque and originally the Belgian training ship *L'Avenir.*

Albert Rickmers. — Steel three-masted barque. This is a good example of the modern three-mast barque, she is perhaps better remembered as *Penang.*

Almirante Saldanha. — Brazilian training ship. This beautiful four masted barquentine is a fine example of the combination of the old sailing ship and modern equipment and fittings.

Archibald Russell. — Steel four-mast barque. A very well-known unit of the grain fleet and a frequent visitor to this country in the last days of sail.

Carl Vinnen. — Steel auxiliary five-mast two-topsail schooner.

Comte de Smet de Naeyer. — Ship. This Belgian training ship was one of the largest of her kind to be ship-rigged.

Coriolanus. — Iron full-rigged ship. The *Coriolanus* was known as "Queen of the Jute Clippers" and is said to have been one of the most beautiful iron ships ever turned out.

Cromdale. — Steel full-rigged ship. A very fine example of one of the later day wool clippers.

Cutty Sark.—Ship. Plans are available for a small scale and relatively simple model of this famous ship.

Danmark. — Ship. This Danish training ship is well known both in this country and also in America, under whose flag she served during World War II.

Discovery. — Wood auxiliary steam barque. This particular set is not claimed to be correct in detail for Captain Scott's famous ship, as at the time the drawings were compiled the actual vessel was not available.

Eagle. — This well known American training ship was originally the German barque *Horst Wessel*, sister ship of the first *Gorch Fock*.

Emma Ernest. — Wood three-mast topsail schooner. A typical coaster and a vessel well-known to Londoners as the *Seven Seas*, moored off the Embankment.

Endeavour. — Bark (1768) this is Captain Cook's famous vessel and these drawings are very fully detailed as the result of careful research work, and really authentic and suitable for perfect scale models.

Falken. — A yacht like schooner-rigged Swedish training ship, which would make a very good sailing model and ideal for plank-on-frame construction.

Fame. — Composite brig. This is one of the Bengal pilot brigs. (See Hoogly pilot brig).

Formby. — Steel-full-rigged ship. Reputed to have been the first vessel to be constructed of steel.

France (II.). — Steel auxiliary five-mast barque. This, the second fivemast barque of that name, was the largest sailing craft ever built.

Georg Stage I. — Ship. This interesting little training ship was originally a steam auxiliary, and these plans show her as built.

Gladan. — Sister ship of the Swedish training schooner *Falken*.

Gorch Fock (I.) — Barque. Sister ship of the American training ship *Eagle* and one of the fine fleet of training ships built by Germany between the two wars.

Grossherzog Friedrich August. — Barque. This beautiful German training ship was built just prior to World War I, and is perhaps one of the most shapely of her kind. She is now the *Statsraad Lehmkuhl*, and a small scale set of plans showing her under that name is also available.

Halcyon. — Steel lee-board ketch. The *Halcyon* is a modern coasting ketch of the barge type.

Harriet MacGregor. — Famous Tasmanian clipper barque, well-known for her passages between Tasmania and London.

Helen Barnet Gring. — A typical American four-mast fore and aft schooner.

Herzogin Cecilie. — Four-masted barque. This vessel needs no introduction, she will be well remembered both as training ship and grain ship.

Joseph Conrad. — Ship. The last square-rigged training ship to wear the British flag. She will be well remembered for her round-the-world cruise under command of her owner, Alan Villiers, with whose assistance these plans have been compiled from the original yard details.

Juan Sebastian De Elcano. — Steel four-mast topsail schooner. This Spanish training ship was designed in Great Britain and is an extremely fine looking craft and an excellent subject for a model.

Kommodore Johnsen. — Steel auxiliary four-masted barque, ex *Magdalene Vinnen* and one of the best known training ships in the last days of sail.

Lady Daphne. — 200-ton Thames sailing barge. This is a typical example of the large coasting barge so well known on the South coast.

Lady of Avenel. — This delightful little wood brigantine was at one time well known trading round the British coast. Later she was fitted out as an ocean-going yacht, and also used for training cruises. It is this later period which is represented by the plans, although her layout was really unchanged except for the large deckhouse and additional boats.

L'Avenir. — Four-masted barque. This is another beautiful vessel which will be well remembered, not only as the fine training ship she was, but also for her later service in the grain fleet. This set of plans includes separate drawings of all deck fittings and mast and spar details.

Leon. — Wood brigantine. This is a particularly pleasing brigantine of the larger class, with raised quarterdeck and trunk cabin. This set also includes a full construction plan for a Plank-on-Frame model and is the basis of this book.

Loch Etive. — Iron full-rigged ship. One of the famous "Loch Line" clippers.

Loch Sunnart. — Iron full-rigged ship. Sister ship of *Loch Etive.*

Magdalene Vinnen (II.). — Steel auxiliary four-mast barque. This is the second four-mast barque of that name and is a typical modern ship with mid-ship bridge deck.

Marie Sophie. — Wood brig. The *Marie Sophie* is a good example of the trading brig in her prime.

Muirneag. — Zulu type fishing vessel. These drawings consist of a full set of constructional plans for the actual vessel. The original drawings were produced by the author for presentation to the Society for Nautical Research as detailed record of this almost extinct type, and were compiled from a full survey of the ship.

Mount Stewart. — Steel full-rigged ship. Sister ship of *Cromdale.*

Mozart. — Steel four-mast barquentine. A well-known and typical example of the modern steel barquentine.

Nippon Maru. — Four-masted barque. This big auxiliary training ship and her sister *Kaiwo Maru* would make fine subjects for model work.

Oamaru. — Iron full-rigged ship. This was one of the famous colonial clippers, and a good looking ship, with long poop and fine lines.

Parma. — Steel four-masted barque, well remembered as regular grain trader to this country, and the subject of Alan Villiers' well-known book of ship photographs, *Last of the Wind Ships.*

Penang. — Steel three-mast barque. (Ex-*Albert Rickmers*).

Pommern. — Steel four-mast barque. Another old friend and regular visitor with the grain ships.

Queen Margaret.—Steel four-mast barque, referred to by Lubbock as "one of the fastest and most beautiful carriers of the nineties".

Raven. — Wood brigantine. A good example of the trading brigantine once so common in both off shore and coasting trades.

Ross-Shire. — Steel four-mast barque. A well remembered member of Thomas Law's fleet of sailing ships.

Runnymede. — Wood snow. This is an interesting old stager with square stern and single topsails.

Statsraad Lehmkuhl. — Steel three-mast barque. A typical modern training ship.

Three Brothers. — Rye smack. Ketch rigged.

Timaru. — Iron full-rigged ship. Sister ship to the iron clipper *Oamaru.*

Torrens. — Composite ship. Well-known as the favourite ship of Joseph Conrad.

True Briton. — This famous Blackwaller would make a fine subject for model making.

Valerian. — Brixham trawler. This is a very comprehensive set with a view to providing all possible details of these fine boats.

Waterwitch. — Wood three-mast barquentine. Another old favourite of the British coast, she was the last real square-rigger on the coast.

William Ashburner. — Three-masted topsail-schooner, one of the last sailing ships in our coastal trade and still well remembered.

COASTING KETCH. — A full set of plans for a trader such as used to be a feature of our small ports and harbours.

COASTING SCHOONER. — This is a typical two-mast Topsail-schooner.

SCANDINAVIAN BARQUENTINE. — This is one of the beautiful little Baltic barquentines which used to be regular visitors to this country.

74-GUN SHIP. — These plans, to a scale of 3/16 in. to 1 ft., are perhaps the most complete set of drawings ever published of one of these old two deckers. The set includes profile, longitudinal and many cross sections; end views, and plans of each deck. There are also separate drawings of each component forming the various masts and spars, together with the position of blocks, rigging sequence and the lead of the gear. Alternative rigging plans are available, one with sails bent and the other for models with bare yards and the lighter gear rigged down. Details of guns, boats, anchors, etc., are also available. These are plans of the actual ship, not simplified model drawings.

HOOGLY PILOT BRIG. — These brigs will be remembered by all who served in the Calcutta trade in the days of sail, and the plans, which are to a scale of l/8 in.=1 ft. 0 in., are from the original builders drawings

SCOTTISH ZULU. — The Zulu was perhaps the finest of all Scottish fishing types, and these plans, to a scale of 1/2 in.= 1 ft. 0 in., were compiled by the author for preservation by the Society for Nautical Research, They are full constructional drawings of the *Muirneag*, taken off the actual vessel while she was being broken up, and when many constructional details otherwise hidden were exposed. Full fitting-out specifications are included, as well as many notes and sketches. A model from these plans is included in this book.

12-GUN BRIG OF WAR. — This set has been produced for super detail ¼ in. scale models of one of the old 12-gun brigs, which many will remember as sail training ships in the Royal Navy.

40-GUN FRIGATE. — The frigate was the cruiser of the Sailing Navy, and these plans are extremely fully detailed and suitable for the construction of a perfect scale model.

THREE-MASTED TOPSAIL SCHOONER. — Drawings of a typical schooner in her clipper days.

ELIZABETHAN GALLEON. — Suitable for a small decorative model, typical of the Elizabethan period.

M.F.V. (MOTOR FISHING VESSEL). — These plans were used for the construction of the plank-built model shown in *Fig.* 27, although in this example the superstructure has been modified by the builder.

RING NET BOAT. — One of the modern cruiser-sterned fishermen of the

Scottish coast. A Plank-on-Frame example of this boat is included among the illustrations in this book. (*Figs.* 22 *and* 23).

SHIP'S BOATS. — A range of details including lines, section, construction plans and details of ships' boats as carried by the sailing man-of-war.

MUZZLE LOADING GUNS. — A range of old time muzzle loading guns as carried in the days of sail.

The above list will of course be added to from time to time.

Particulars of plans on application to: Brown, Son & Ferguson, Ltd., 4-10 Darnley St., Glasgow G41 2SD

INDEX

PLANK-ON-FRAME MODELS

INDEX

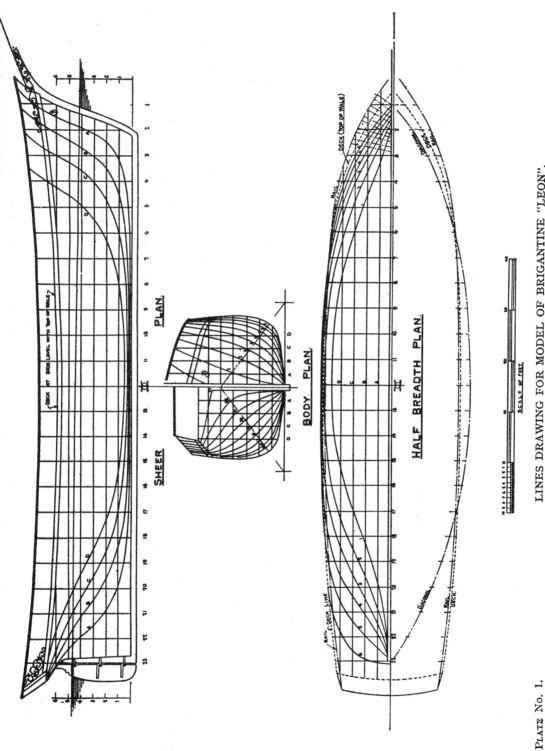

LINES DRAWING FOR MODEL OF BRIGANTINE "LEON".
Showing location of cant-frames.

PLATE No. 1.

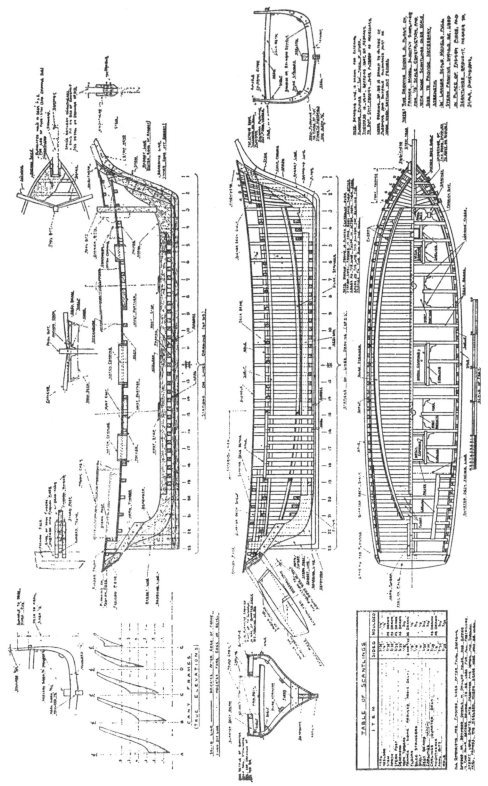

PLATE No. 2.　　CONSTRUCTION PLAN FOR 1/8 in. SCALE MODEL OF BRIGANTINE "LEON".

(Built-up frame Construction)

(Reduced from full-size plans of model)

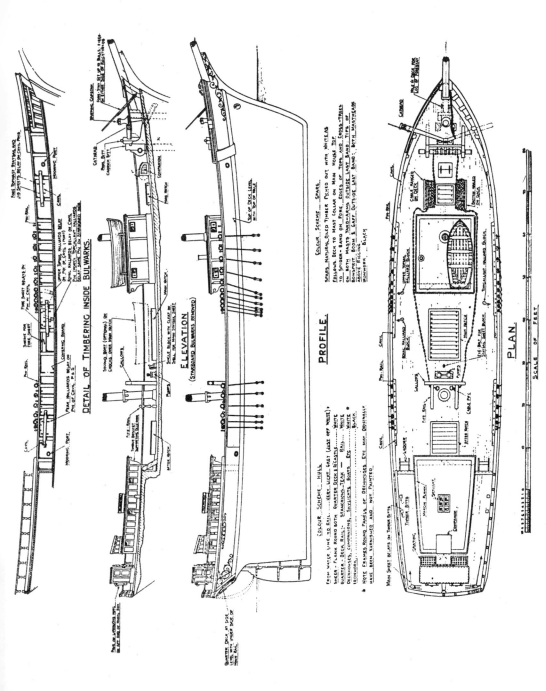

PLATE No 3. DECK PLAN AND PROFILES, 1/8 in. SCALE MODEL OF BRIGANTINE "LEON."
(Reduced from full-size plans of model.)

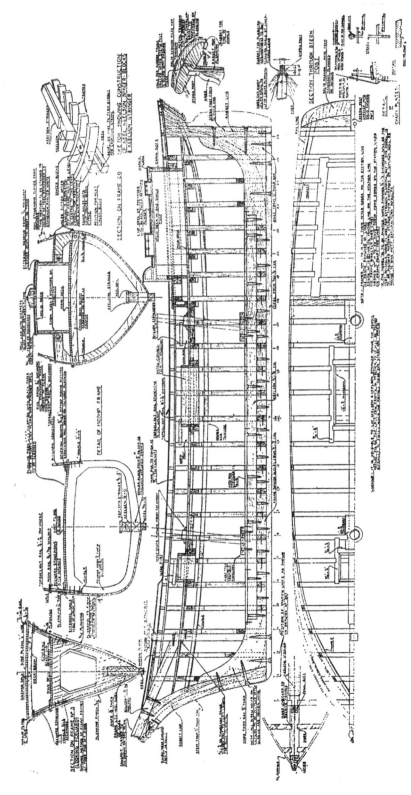

PLATE No. 4.   CONSTRUCTION PLAN FOR 1/4 in. SCALE MODEL OF BRIG "MARIE SOPHIE".

(Reduced from full-size plans of model)   (Sawn-out frame Construction).

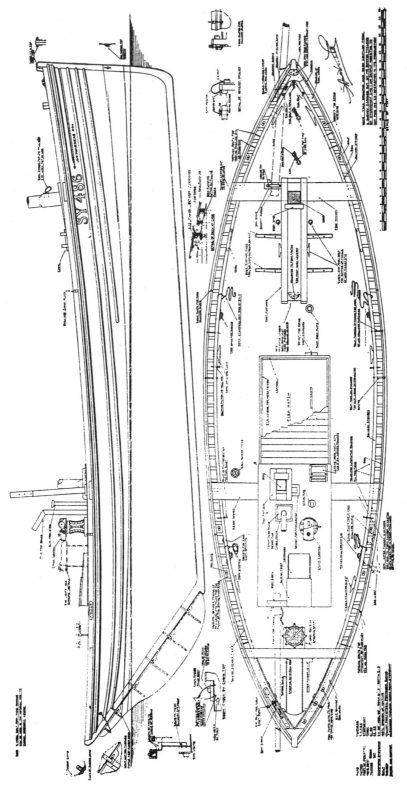

PLATE No. 5.

(Reduced from ¼" scale plans of vessel.)

PROFILE AND DECK PLAN OF ZULU "MUIRNEAG".

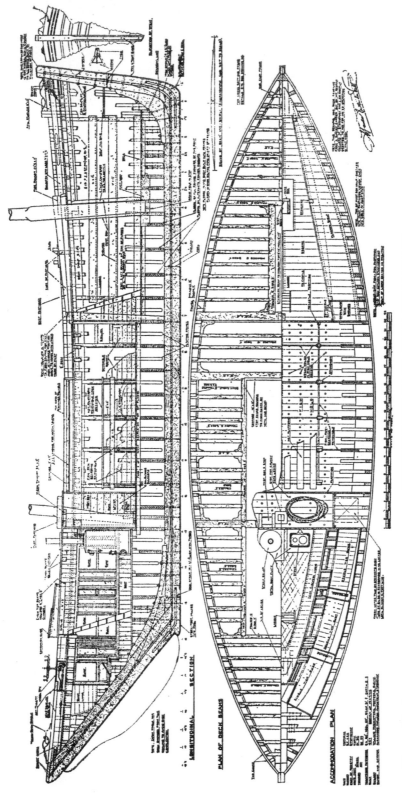

PLATE No 6.

(Reduced from ¾" scale plans of vessel)

CONSTRUCTION PLAN, ZULU "MUIRNEAG".

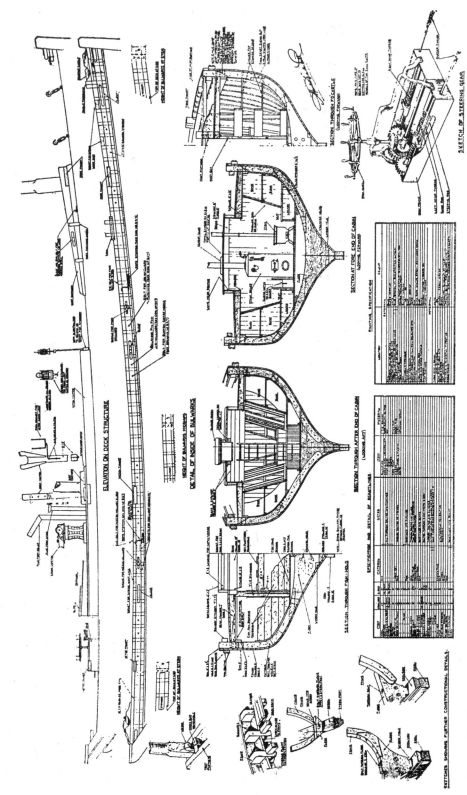

PLATE No. 7.

(Reduced from ¼" scale plans of vessel.)

SECTION AND DETAILS, ZULU "MUIRNEAG".